RANDY ROBISON

UPGRADE

DEVOTIONAL

BREAKFAST
FOR SEVEN

upgrade

transitive verb

---

1) to raise the quality of;

2) to replace something with a more useful version or alternative

Contents

DO YOU WANT SOMETHING BETTER THAN WHAT YOU HAVE?

In a relatively short amount of time, you can learn to upgrade every area of your life. But here's the thing about upgrades: It's not always about going from *bad* to *good*. It's usually about going from *good* to *even better*. We understand this in our daily lives. When cell phones came out, it was revolutionary. But when smartphones came out . . . well, we all had to have one. We upgraded.

If you're flying somewhere, and they offer a free upgrade to first class, do you refuse? No way! You'll still arrive at your destination at the same time, but you'll have traveled in style. One time, my sister and her husband gave my wife and me one of those fancy coffee machines that makes cappuccino, espresso, and a dozen other drinks. I threw my old one-cup coffee machine away. Why? Because an upgrade is always better.

What if you could upgrade every aspect of your life? Your thoughts, words, actions, family, work, friends, and even yourself? I'm here to tell you that you can. Don't settle for second-rate. Ditch the landline, fly first class, and drink great coffee!

Whatever shape your life is in, it can get better. And you can have it all for the low, low price of nothing. It's free. There's just one catch. You have to give up the old one. Just like you have to give up your seat in coach to fly first class, you have to leave where you're at now to move up to a better place.

The good news is that it's not complicated. The steps are simple, proven, and straight from an ancient book of wisdom. I am just going to help you walk through them so you can make that glorious exchange and start enjoying the perks immediately.

Get ready. It's time to **UPGRADE.**

WEEK 1

"All that a man achieves and all that he fails to achieve is the direct result of his own thoughts."

—JAMES ALLEN, *As A Man Thinketh*

UPGRADE
Your Thoughts

Heaven and earth witness the choices you make every day, and every choice begins in your mind. What you think determines what you say and what you do. If you say or do something wrong, people are quick to point it out. Disciplinary action may be necessary. But nobody can police your thoughts, except you.

The first key to upgrading your life is understanding and believing that much of your health starts in your mind. Right thoughts lead to right words and actions. Focusing on your words and actions alone, without examining your thoughts, only treats the symptom not the disease. Eliminating unhealthy thoughts and replacing them with healthy thoughts will do more to improve your life than almost anything else you can do.

Taking control of your thoughts is more than just harnessing the power of positive thinking. It's also about submitting them to God. Even though God's principles always work, many principles outlined in this book will work without fully acknowledging Him because He wrote the rules of the universe and created mankind.

However, your thought life will never be perfected or reach its full potential until you admit the ultimate source of all truth, goodness, and righteousness is God. Allowing Him to guide your thoughts enables you to live a life beyond your own ability. The first step to a better life begins with the renewing of your mind, letting God change your mind every day.

DAY 1
Knowledge Is Good

Knowledge is the collection of information. It's like putting data into a computer. The material can be accessed and displayed at any time, but that's all it is: the compilation of information. The more we learn, the more knowledge we have. Learning doesn't stop when we finish school. In many ways, it just begins. Every day, we can learn something new.

Have you ever argued with an atheist? I have. I've even read a few of the modern "classics" by atheists such as Christopher Hitchens, Sam Harris, and Richard Dawkins. I find it quite amusing. I understand those who call themselves *agnostic*—meaning they simply don't know whether God exists or not. Big questions surround the belief in God. But atheism? It's laughable. They argue that one cannot prove God exists, therefore He doesn't. As if human "proof" is the ultimate measure of the universe. For believers in God, it's a matter of faith. We *choose* to believe God exists. However, the same is true for atheists. They cannot prove God does not exist, so they *choose* to believe He doesn't. Again, it's a matter of faith.

No single person or collection of people have all knowledge of all things. Or, as my pastor puts it, "We're all ignorant, just in different areas." Even the experts have gaps in their chosen field.

Oceanographers don't know everything that lives in the depths. Astronomists continuously discover previously unknown stars, planets, and even universes. Doctors are constantly changing how they treat their patients, because there is still so much we don't know about the human body. This pursuit of knowledge is essential and good. The moment we think there is nothing more to learn, we are doomed to foolishness. When we stop learning, we don't just cease moving forward, we start sliding backward.

The first step to acquiring knowledge is maintaining an inquisitive mind. That's my beef with atheism: it demands a closed mind. Those who advocate atheism push an enthusiasm without knowledge and make mistakes in their haste. Whenever any of us find contentment in limiting our knowledge or take pride in the mockery of open discussion, we settle for being close-minded.

Second, if you really want to expand your ability to acquire knowledge, acknowledge God first. Respect His position as Creator of everything. After all, if He made it, He has knowledge of it. This extends to every area of life.

A scientist who wants to unlock the secrets of our world can ask the original Engineer who built it. The business owner who needs to know how to run a successful enterprise and cultivate a healthy workplace can ask the CEO who owns everything and knows every heart. A mother who wants to raise good children can ask the perfect Father how to instruct them. There is no limit to knowledge when we tap into the limitless, divine Knower of all things.

Third, gaining knowledge demands discipline. A little information can be misleading. I have read a few articles on quantum physics, but I'm not about to teach a course on it. I see this tendency in our internet-driven news these days. People read headlines but not the articles. Often, the headlines convey something incomplete or even contradictory to the real story. People that feed on this have information, but are of no real use.

UPGRADE
Your Thoughts

In May of 2018, President Trump was speaking at a roundtable on border security, and Sheriff Margaret Mimms of Fresno County, California, brought up the problem of violent MS-13 gang members coming in from Central America. In his response to Sheriff Mimms, he called them "animals." Someone on Twitter edited the video to remove the gang reference and claimed the president was talking about all immigrants. The Associated Press initially ran with it then retracted it. Other media outlets continued to repeat the slander. Almost a year later, presidential candidates for 2020 were still railing against the sitting president calling immigrants "animals," just days after MS-13 had brutally stabbed and burned the body of one of their own in Virginia. I tell this story simply to illustrate how we must have the discipline to push past the noise of information flooding us and take hold of the totality of facts, and within context—not fall victim to specious claims.

When a couple is having marital problems, it's common to have three sides to the issue: his side, her side, and the truth. To receive help, a third-party person must hear both sides and discern the truth, which is typically somewhere in between his and her version. A little information can lead to bias, misinformation, or wrong conclusions. Knowledge alone is a good start, but it's only the beginning.

Pursuing knowledge makes you smarter, and intelligent people actively learn. Make it a lifelong habit to unearth nuggets of truth, discard the fool's gold of lies and half-truths, and store up knowledge. Then take it to the next level so it can become useful to your life.

DAY 2
Understanding Is Better

Once we gather knowledge, we must take it a step further with *understanding*. This is the ability to take meaning from facts. How do they relate to each other? What truths can be drawn from them? It requires a level of thinking beyond memorization. With proper understanding, principles can be constructed, rules can be made, and life can become navigable. It's the difference between observing that the sky is dark and there's a loud rumble (both facts) and knowing that it's about to storm (understanding). Knowledge incorporates our senses—what we see, hear, taste, touch, and smell—while understanding requires the mind.

The process of understanding can be found in an unlikely place: schlocky crime novels. The formula goes like this: A rough-at-the-edges detective defies an arrogant captain, gets fired, then has to run down a trail of clues involving rich widows, corrupt businessmen, and shady barroom characters. He gets tips from a rookie cop and his loyal friend in the morgue to solve the crime. The killer goes to the electric chair, the jerk of a captain gets fired, and our hero gets reinstated in the police department. You know the type.

A good novel strings out information that the detective must sift through to gain understanding. He must sort out the truths, half-truths, lies, misunderstandings, things that look one way but really lean another, and so forth. The honorable detective also stays sober, follows the facts where they lead, and refuses to cross certain lines in order to avoid becoming just as crooked as the rest of the characters.

That's the first point: to gain understanding. And you must make a conscious effort to do right. (Yes, you can get a good point from a worn-out plot!) Gaining facts to fit your agenda only works if your agenda is pure and inherently correct, which is rare. Gaining facts to form your view and allowing truth to take you where it leads are smarter approaches.

Improperly applying facts can have devastating real-life consequences. Just ask Timothy Bridges of North Carolina. He spent over 25 years in prison for a rape and burglary he did not commit. After an elderly woman was robbed and badly beaten, about 10 months went by without any leads. Then three police informants, all with prior criminal records, claimed Bridges had confessed to them. He consistently maintained his innocence, but police charged him with the crimes. The victim, who had been wheelchair-bound and in poor health even before the vicious attack, died before the trial began. She never gave a reliable physical description of her attacker. However, she insisted that she was not raped, but a physician claimed she probably was. An FBI-trained crime lab employee testified that two hairs found at the crime scene had to belong to Bridges. The bloody palm print found at the crime scene did not match Bridges' print, but the crime lab testimony was enough to lock him away for life. Decades later, it was discovered that the testimony was "scientifically unsound." The science that locked up an innocent man was wrong. Two hairs, wrongly identified, cost him half his life.

Bridges' case was overturned, and he walked out of prison on October 1, 2015. Two years later, the city of Charlotte agreed to pay him a record $9.5 million for the wrongful rape conviction but refused to admit any wrongdoing. They didn't even apologize. Facts are not always enough. If wrongly interpreted or applied, you get wrong results. Wrong results can hurt people. But proper understanding can help people. God knows that would have drastically changed Tim Bridges' life. It also would have helped the family of the victim, and it would have saved Charlotte taxpayers millions of dollars. Of course, it also should have put the real criminal in jail. If only someone in that case had proper understanding, it would have prevented a lot of pain and given justice to the elderly victim.

You probably won't be called upon to exercise your understanding in order to determine someone else's fate, but you are called every day to exercise understanding in order to determine your own fate. Charles Spurgeon said, "There is no fool so great a fool as a knowing fool." Gathering knowledge is the first step but certainly not the final step. It is common to know something yet respond foolishly.

This plays out every day in situations far more mundane than a detective novel or real-life criminal case. Someone at work may be short with you, but you can only speculate why. Stopping with the knowledge that he or she said something rude can lead to resentment. Assuming it was your fault can lead to shame. Complaining to others about it is mere gossip. If appropriate, you could press for more information. The possibilities are endless. Perhaps your co-worker is not feeling well. Maybe he or she is dealing with a family crisis. Whatever the issue, gaining an understanding of the situation puts you in a better position to deal with it. If you did something to warrant the attitude, you may need to apologize and make corrections. If there is a personal crisis in that person's life, you may be able to help.

Taking a proactive approach instead of merely reacting to others empowers you to make positive changes wherever you are.

Gather the information you need to gain better understanding, and you will think more clearly—solving problems instead of passing them by or making them worse. Develop Godly understanding and you will be happier, more successful, and favored by others. It will be a fountain of life to you.

DAY 3
Wisdom Is Best

There's a difference between knowledge, understanding, and wisdom. The pinnacle of Godly thought is wisdom. Moving to this highest level of thinking and living benefits you more than any amount of money—yet most of us spend our lives working for the next paycheck. But are we better off working 40 hours a week for "silver and gold" or spending that time on something that will yield better results? Fortunately, it's not an either/or situation. It just requires going to work. Not "going to a job," but going to work on our hearts and minds. And just like we get paid for working, we reap the rewards of pursuing wisdom. So, what exactly is wisdom?

Once you have the facts (knowledge) and derive proper meaning from it (understanding), what do you do with it? This is where wisdom comes in. Remember the storm? Fact: It's cloudy. Fact: There's thunder. Meaning: It's likely to storm. And then you stand outside and get hit by lightning. Why? Because you lacked wisdom!

Wisdom says, "Take shelter." It absorbs the facts, understands the meaning, and leads you on the best course of action. Most people manage to gather some of the facts. We call these folks "smart." Many learn to apply those facts in some way. We call them "experts." But few really figure out how to apply their knowledge and understanding across all areas of life. I suppose we could call those people "rare."

Surely, you've seen this by now. Someone who's brilliant in some way does something that seems obviously stupid. A politician hires a prostitute only to be discovered by a reporter. A businessman deletes a hard drive only to have it recovered. A pastor sleeps with his secretary. Dumb, even though they knew the facts and understood what would happen when discovered.

Wisdom is by far the most valuable thing we can develop mentally, and subsequently apply practically. It's better than all the money in the world. Just ask a few formerly rich people.

Sadly, professional athletes are prone to going from poor to very rich to poor again. It happens in a society that rewards physical ability with the kind of cash most of us can't imagine. A quick look at some of Forbes' top 100 for 2018 gives you an idea (salary or winnings and endorsements combined):

- #1 Floyd Mayweather (boxing)—$285 million
- #2 Lionel Messi (soccer)—$111 million
- #4 Conor McGregor (mixed martial arts)—$99 million
- #6 LeBron James (basketball)—$85.5 million
- #7 Roger Federer (tennis)—$77.2 million
- #9 Matt Ryan (football)—$67.3 million
- #12 Lewis Hamilton (auto racing)—$51 million
- #16 Tiger Woods (golf)—$43.3 million

At the "bottom" of the list are a bunch of guys I've never heard of, pulling in $20+ million for the year. That's some serious dough. (The smartest? #45 Usain Bolt. The only track star on the list. Won $1 million in running. Earned $30 million in endorsements. Brilliant!)

Hopefully these guys will all live within their means, invest well, be generous, and plan for the future; but historically, that hasn't always been the case. People who are often from modest backgrounds and get big athletic paydays usually are not prepared to handle it. They've been focused on the physical not the financial. When they get the big payday, they are instantly rich. They can buy anything they want. Everyone is their friend. And every past acquaintance, distant family member, and fast-talking money manager wants a piece of it. Without wisdom, the athlete has no chance at all. That money is as good as gone. The real value is not in the big contract; it's in the wisdom needed to handle it.

Wisdom brings its own reward. Sometimes it's financial, but it's always much more, which is why it's better than riches. God's blessing is on wisdom itself, so when you gain wisdom, you gain blessing. Even in the church, we seem to lose sight of this truth. We spend more time working for money and praying for blessings, when attention to acquiring wisdom would bring both.

We are told very little about Jesus' childhood, but Luke notes that He kept "increasing in wisdom." When He did start His ministry, those who witnessed it asked, "Where did this man get this wisdom and these miraculous powers?" (Matthew 13:54 NIV.) You'd think that miracles would command the spotlight. It's impressive when a blind man is healed! Yet right there with physical occurrences that defy explanation is a quality that's invisible, yet just as remarkable. Wisdom is that significant.

Wisdom is strength. In fact, it's more powerful than the strong. In cases of war, strength fights the battle, but wisdom directs the forces. If not, it's a recipe for disaster. A general can have the biggest army in the world and the most powerful weapons ever manufactured, but if he does not know how to use them, he will be defeated. The same is true mentally. We can have an array of facts and the most powerful means to disseminate knowledge, but without wisdom, the only outcome will be failure.

Wisdom nourishes your soul. Spiritually, it has more nutritional value than the most vitamin-rich food and is sweeter than your favorite dessert. It will sustain you, make you sharper, maintain your mental health, and carry you through each day. It also gives you hope for the future. No matter what hardship or setback you may face, you can see a way forward. Knowledge will rescue you; understanding will enable you; and wisdom will direct you.

Perhaps the best news of all is that wisdom is freely given. Just ask. (See James 1:5.) You do need to ask daily, because that's how often we need it. You need not unlock any secrets, attain some level of perfection, or belong to a certain church. Just ask. Not only will God give it to you, but He *wants* to give it to you. Every minute of every day.

DAY 4
Seek Good Advice

We were not made to go through life alone. God made Eve for Adam. He made a nation of the Israelites, when nations were defined by people groups rather than topographical borders. Jesus made brothers out of a band of 12 men. The first century church started fellowships in homes in an expanding roster of cities, appointing trusted believers to positions of responsibility and authority. People were created for community.

An important part of gaining wisdom taps into that community by seeking the advice of wise (which means Godly) people. That's why it's essential to put some of these people in your inner circle. All of us have people around us who will give bad advice—that can't be avoided. So it is necessary to intentionally position some wise advisors close. Those may come naturally, whether family members, church leaders, or possibly co-workers. If there are no candidates around you, it will require some work. It's worth the search, because when you have these people in your inner circle, they can help you in many ways.

First, they help us plan. A great idea can crash quickly with poor execution. That's why any significant endeavor—choosing a school, selecting a mate, starting a business, changing jobs, moving to a new place—needs forethought. Planning leads to prosperity, but haste leads to failure. Setting goals, plotting a course, and refining execution along the way enables success. Rushing into something without thinking it through is a recipe for disaster. That's probably the biggest reason businesses fail, marriages break up, frustration sets in, and difficulty ensues. Getting sage advice on the front end can save you so much trouble. Wise people can speak from their experiences to help us avoid their mistakes and emulate their victories. They often provide valuable connections, putting us in touch with other people and organizations that can assist us, partner with us, and guide us. Plans may change, but that's okay. Ups and downs are a natural part of anything that succeeds. However, if we do not plan, we condemn ourselves to unnecessary wandering, stumbling, and likely failing.

Second, wise people can spot potential trouble. We can't always see beyond our circumstances, especially when we are feeling pressure. Stress clouds our vision. Reacting to it blinds us to pitfalls that someone else might easily foresee, so having another perspective gives us another set of eyes. If there's a hole in our plan or an unseen danger, a good advisor can raise the red flag. Even when our plan is solid—untainted by anxiety or a lack of information—an outside angle can strengthen us further. Avoiding trouble saves pain and allows us to achieve our goals quicker.

Third, good advisors help make sure our ideas fit us as unique individuals. By this, I mean that not all decisions are inherently wrong; they just may not be the best course of action for you. This type of counsel can be particularly difficult to hear because what we plan may not be wrong. It just may not fit as well as another course. The choice between multiple good options can be one of the most difficult to make, because there's no bad choice. That's why Godly advice is not just about right and wrong; it's about finding God's best for each of us individually. When you have someone in your inner circle that speaks on this level, don't feel slighted. Feel honored. It shows how much God cares about every aspect of your life. As we spiritually mature, we move beyond simply right or wrong. We move into good or best.

Here's the thing about good advice: We have to take it. Solomon, who wrote most of the book of Proverbs and is considered the wisest man in the Bible, didn't even take his own advice. The same man who wrote long passages warning young men about the destruction of being enticed by lust had 700 wives and 300 concubines! Many of them were not Israelites, so they worshiped false gods and led him astray. The latter part of his life is recorded with this sad observation: "For when Solomon was old, his wives turned his heart away after other gods; and his heart was not wholly devoted to the Lord his God . . ." (1 Kings 11:4 NASB).

Even the wisest among us are subject to the consequences of ignoring good advice. Likewise, we walk a dangerous road when we always think we are right, while the Godly people in our lives have warned us of our folly. The one who thinks everyone else is wrong is typically the fool. Spurning good advice begs for trouble, but listening to others who have wisdom increases our own. It takes humility to hear wise words and act on them. Pride will only close our ears to truth and set us on a path to ruin. However, learning to listen to good advice leads to a lifetime of wisdom. Make it a point to gather wise advisors around you and hear them out.

DAY 5
Take Correction

Perhaps the hardest thing to learn from is criticism. Critics can be merciless, unfair, and mean. In today's age of social media drama, most critics should be ignored. But there comes a point when critics can be right, especially if they offer correction in a spirit of redemption.

I've witnessed many high-profile religious leaders—people whose names you would know—being privately called out for wrongdoing by other religious leaders. Few have listened. The ones who have heeded the wisdom of others are still in ministry, doing well in their calling. Those who dismissed correction simply as negative criticism, or even ungodly voices, eventually fell. Sometimes publicly. The phrase "if only he had listened" has been uttered too many times.

I get it. Criticism and correction—even when constructive—is difficult to hear. Nobody likes to be on the receiving end. It can be hard to know if it's legitimate. There are instances throughout history when one person stood against a tide of injustice or evil, but that's rare. In most cases, pride stands in the way of hearing correction. In ministry, it can even be spiritual pride.

When I was in college at Oral Roberts University, a local pastor had become a bit of a star. His church grew rapidly, and when he spoke at conferences, people came to listen. He lit it up. He was gifted, delivered a great message, and energized the crowd. I had the privilege of knowing him personally. He invited me to his condo for dinner. He was a really cool guy.

After I graduated, he called me one day and asked me to listen to a couple of sermons he had preached. I took two cassette tapes (yeah, I know) on a road trip and listened to both sermons twice. He was preaching something I hadn't heard before, though it wasn't anything new. People were starting to call it heresy. I didn't know what to think. I was young, though biblically literate, and it sounded appealing; but I couldn't align it with Scripture. In short, it was what has been called "Christian universalism," meaning that everyone has been saved by Christ—they just may not know it yet.

We had lunch shortly after I returned and discussed the topic. I told him that I couldn't reconcile it with the Bible, even though it sounded compassionate and alluring. I asked him if he had discussed it with anyone else. He retrieved a letter from Oral Roberts himself. Oral had been a mentor of his, so this pastor had sought his advice. He read the letter, and it was beautiful. Oral Roberts gently, but firmly, refuted the idea in the way a father would correct his son. I nodded and said, "That's it. He's spot on."

Sadly, my pastor friend didn't listen. He decided that we, and almost every other voice in his life, were all wrong. He continued preaching this message, which meant his friends in ministry could no longer invite him to speak at their conferences. His church fell apart. He painted himself as a martyr and separated from all wise counsel in his life. He led many people down an unorthodox path, cherry-picking Scriptures and ignoring the whole context. That's what happens when you reject wise counsel. You lead people astray. If this pastor had just listened to the people that God had put around him, he could have been showing others the right way.

But he couldn't hear constructive criticism.

You might be tempted to think that religious leaders spurned him simply because he dabbled in errancy. The truth is that those who knew him grieved as he wandered away. If he had shown some willingness to listen and be corrected, he would have been honored and exalted among his peers, as well as in God's eyes. We all make mistakes. We all play the role of the lost sheep, but the love of Jesus Christ is such that He leaves the 99 in the fold to rescue the one. If we only listen to correction and even criticism in a healthy way, God and His people will honor our humility as we return and submit to His authority. In the end, we will be wiser for it.

Conversely, if we reject the counsel, correction, and constructive criticism of Godly people, we show ourselves to be foolish. Obstinance doesn't automatically make us special; it usually makes us stupid. If you find yourself in that position, just weigh what it has brought you. If you have peace and assurance from God, you may be that Noah or Daniel figure. But, if you are sowing a storm, you will reap the whirlwind.

Again, surrounding yourself with good, Godly advisors will help you know the difference. Stay humble, seek wisdom, and take correction. And most of all, listen.

DAY 6
Use Your Brain

Humans tend to be mentally lazy. Christians are not immune to this. But God gave you a brain, so learn to use it. When you gather knowledge, obtain understanding, and receive wisdom, you can rely more on your thought process—always keeping it in check with the Bible and Godly counsel.

Rule number one: Think before you act. I have to tell myself this often—and still it seems it's not often enough! It's easy to react, which usually gets us in trouble. If we practice the think-then-act pattern instead, the world around us will change for the better. It's a bit like proofreading an email before hitting "Send." Mistakes are easy, so take a minute to pause before going through with something. You won't always have a "Recall" button.

Develop a mental checklist, and practice it until it becomes automatic. Ask yourself questions like, *What am I wanting to accomplish with what I'm about to do or say?* This forces an intentionality that is healthy. *Will this word or action achieve what I want to achieve?* Clarity is paramount. Sometimes a lack of forethought creates unintended consequences. *How will it impact others?* Communication is as much about how it's received as how it's delivered. *Is there a better way to say it or do it?* Self-edit before you speak or act. *Is it even necessary?* Often the best course of action is to be still, stay silent, or wait.

These types of questions will safeguard you in so many ways. They will also prevent you from hurting others, whether intentionally or inadvertently. You'll find that it creates self-awareness and sensitivity that benefit you as well as those around you.

Conversely, it's easy to go through each day just doing what we habitually do and saying what pops into our minds. Adding a little thinking—some purpose, wisdom, reflection, and clarity—will make a huge impact. Try it for a while. You may be surprised how much of a difference it makes.

By the way, did you catch it when an ad for a Fisher-Price "Happy Hour Playset" hit the internet? The front of the box portrayed three-year-olds standing around a plastic toy bar, holding fake beer bottles. It spread around social media pretty quickly. Talk about not thinking before acting . . . which is what most people failed to do as they shared the fake post in outrage. It was not real. A comedian made it up and posted it on Instagram. Then it went viral as a "real" thing, which brings me to rule number two: Don't believe everything you hear.

The information age has become the *dis*information age. The easiest thing to do is perpetuate something that is false or misleading with the click of a button. The two biggest drivers are negative emotions, like anger and fear, plus the desire to want something to be true. Don't fall for it. Even if it fits and supports your sense of right and wrong, make sure it's legitimate before you attempt to influence your friends with it. You really don't want to be that person—you know, the one who's always outraged by something that's circumspect or who spreads gossip about things they really don't understand.

The same is true with spiritual things. Just because a Christian leader says something, even with the support of a few phrases out of the Bible, take the time to investigate it on your own if you care enough to spread it. When it comes to Scripture, it's important to know that two things happen: First, we interpret it; second, we apply it. There is only one correct interpretation, but there are many possible applications. When it comes to interpretation, there are good, Godly people who disagree. Don't start calling everyone a heretic if they don't see everything the way you do. Know that someone is right and someone is wrong, but there is only One who is right every time. We need to have the grace to deal with others' imperfections, even as we pursue perfection.

Perhaps the most historic difference in interpretation surrounds Christ's declaration: ". . . upon this rock I will build my church" in Matthew 16:18. The Catholic Church interprets this as meaning the entire church would be built upon one man: Simon Peter, whom they regard as the first pope. All church authority then descends through the papacy. Non-Catholics, or Protestants, interpret that phrase as Christ building the church on divine revelation, which Peter had just exhibited. It's a significant difference, but it's not one worth going to war over. Christ instructed us to love our enemies, so surely we should love believers with a different interpretation of church authority, even while holding to our convictions.

As for application, this is much more fluid, though it should never contradict Scripture or abandon sound principles and methods of interpreting the text. Bad interpretation pretty much always leads to bad application, but even correct interpretation doesn't guarantee flawless application. Scripture is so deep and full of meaning that it can be read for a lifetime and continuously have new application. This is because the Holy Spirit is alive and uses this inspired book to enlighten humanity. Still, it's vital to remember that we do not worship the book; we worship the Author, who has not gone silent. He has given us the written word as a baseline for doctrine, but He will speak through His Word in very personal and specific ways.

If you're wondering about application, ask a couple of simple questions: *Does it make us more like Christ? Does it point others to God?* If it makes us think, speak, or act in a way that does not exhibit love, joy, peace, patience, kindness, goodness, faithfulness, gentleness, and self-control, it's not of God. And if it elevates us over God, it is not of God. As you mature spiritually, you will learn how to discern what is right, but remember that love is the one constant requirement in every disagreement. We are not commanded to agree with everyone, but we are commanded to love them.

Sound thinking and discretion will bring life to your soul and help guide your way. Mental laziness is never acceptable. Iron sharpens iron, so let the hard challenges come. Wrestle with things with humility and grace. Submit your mind to the Lord, then use the brain He gave you.

DAY 7
Stay Focused

I don't recommend driving with one eye covered. I speak from experience. Both of my retinas have detached, though a few years apart. Fortunately, they can fix that, but it often causes cataracts to form, which happened in both eyes. I have had a few surgeries, which means I'm familiar with an eye patch.

When you're down to one eye, you lose depth perception, which is why driving becomes a bit of a challenge. Lane markers become critical, just to keep you centered on the road. Radio controls on the steering wheel make life safer and easier because you can surf the stations while keeping one good eye on traffic. When your vision is limited or damaged, staying focused takes extra effort.

The same is true in life. Hardships can blind us. Limitations prevent us from seeing everything at once. Distractions cause us to drift off course. Developing the discipline to maintain focus becomes critical. Without it, we may never get where we want to go.

Pay attention to where you are going in life, as well as where you want to go. Set goals and keep your eyes on them. This is your path to achievement and fulfillment. Of course, this assumes you have God-given goals. If not, spend more time gathering knowledge, obtaining understanding, and increasing in wisdom. By doing so, you'll establish these God-given goals. Once you have established them, maintain focus in achieving them with this one very important caveat: detours.

If you have ever moved to a new location, whether a big city or a small town, you know the frustration that happens when you try to navigate your way around. Frankly, the reason I know my way around several different cities is because I've gotten lost. A lot. Ironically, the technology that helps prevent that these days also creates drivers who don't have a clue where they are or how to get where they want to go. If their smartphone ever fails to say, "Turn here," they don't have a squirrel's chance in rush hour. And if a detour pops up due to unforeseen circumstances, a familiar route becomes an adventure into uncharted territory. When this happens, stay calm and stay focused. Just take the time to learn along the way. I've found some great new restaurants by getting lost!

Failures can become valuable learning experiences, even though time can be lost to them. Maintaining focus on the overall goal will get you through dead ends, U-turns, delays, and detours. Don't let the distraction or discouragement break your focus. Use them to gain information, knowledge, and wisdom. Lessons from the past will enable you to better navigate the future.

The key component to maintaining focus through every situation is vision—not just the metaphorical kind that allows us to see where we want our goals and dreams to take us, but the spiritual kind—the ability to see the things of God that our natural eyes cannot see. This is not an excuse to live in a fantasy of our own making, but it is a call to step into what God has put into motion by the redemption brought through Jesus Christ and the fulfillment of His plans on earth. It's illustrated by the Kingdom of God, which simply means the extension of His rule over the hearts of mankind. His prayer is that His will be done on earth as it is done in heaven (see Matthew 6:10). Once spiritually reborn, we are invited to take a role in the fulfillment of this prayer, which is more than a wish but a divine play being acted out on the stage of history. Seeing it gives life meaning, purpose, and design.

Kingdom is a major theme in the Bible. John the Baptist preached that "the kingdom of heaven is at hand" (see Matthew 3:2). Jesus said the same thing when he began preaching. In Luke 4, He said that preaching the Kingdom of God was His *purpose*. Many of His parables were designed to illustrate what the Kingdom of God looked like. After the resurrection, He spent 40 days with His disciples ". . . speaking of the things concerning the kingdom of God" (Acts 1:3 NASB). The book of Acts leaves us with Paul ". . . testifying about the kingdom of God" (Acts 28:23 NASB).

Embrace your role as an ambassador of His Kingdom, inviting others with your words and actions to find their place in His Kingdom. In the broadest sense, this is our purpose: living under His lordship and expanding His Kingdom. How that plays out in your life is as unique and individual as you are. Focusing on hearing His voice and acting on His direction enable you to fulfill that privileged role.

Life is full of distractions that will try to pull you left or right. The world bombards you with them non-stop. When you find yourself distracted by something that detracts from God's goal and purpose for your life, shut it down. Turn it off, tune it out, disable the app . . . whatever it takes. If these distractions are sinful, rooting them out will bring you the stability you desperately need. If you think you can hold on to sin and still fulfill your purpose and achieve your goals, your thinking is jacked up. That kind of rationale will make you unstable in everything you do. Get rid of it, and rewire your mind by renewing your mind with the Word (see Roman 12:2). You will find yourself happier and more fulfilled when you eliminate anything that interferes with your God-ordained purpose.

Take intentional steps. Make moves with purpose. Don't react in reply to your circumstances; act in response to your calling. The rudder determines the direction of a sailboat, but winds move it. Without a rudder, that boat drifts aimlessly. The winds of life will push us, so we need something below the surface to channel the forces around us into a purposeful direction. When we pay attention to the things we do, putting God's plans into action, there are no accidents or coincidences. There is the movement of God through our lives.

Finally, never give up. The legendary football coach Vince Lombardi said, "It's not whether you get knocked down; it's whether you get up." When you fall, get back up again. Life will knock you down; that's a given. Don't waste energy complaining about it or feeling sorry for yourself. Enlist the help of others if you cannot stand on your own. Remember, the loser of a fight isn't the one who gets knocked down; it's the one who stays down.

The Old Testament is full of stories of people who got knocked down, either by their actions or the actions of others. Joseph was enslaved. David committed adultery. Moses murdered a guy. Why didn't they fall away into the dustbin of failures? Because they got back up and answered God's call on their lives. Success isn't measured by how many times you fail; it's measured by how many times you accept His correction and choose to obey. We all disqualify ourselves from fulfilling God's plan for our lives. Fortunately, it does not rest on us. We can't qualify ourselves, so our self-disqualification is meaningless when seen in the light of His qualification. Don't give up. Not now, not ever. Stay focused.

WEEK 2

"Words . . . how potent for good and evil they become in the hands of one who knows how to combine them."

—NATHANIEL HAWTHORNE

UPGRADE
Your Words

I *n our social media world, words have become cheaper than ever. Anyone with a smartphone can sound off and the whole world can read it. Most ignore it. Yet words can have tremendous impact for good or evil.*

One of the greatest speeches ever delivered is President Abraham Lincoln's Gettysburg Address. A scant 272 words, it took him less than three minutes to deliver it. Yet those words, commemorated in stone at the Lincoln Memorial in Washington D.C., inspire people today. But did you know that another speaker preceded the president's famous address?

Edward Everett had risen through the political ranks in Boston and Washington D.C. to become secretary of state. His reputation as a brilliant orator earned him the honor of speaking before President Lincoln at Gettysburg that day. For two hours, he delivered a rousing speech. Nobody remembers it.

Words have power but only when used to convey powerful ideas with clarity and concision. In our world of endless words, there is little real power because the words are meaningless, unpersuasive, unclear, or unheard. Yet you can rise above the clutter of average by mastering your tongue and its secretary— your hands. When you train your brain with better thoughts, the next logical step is to learn how to effectively express those idea to others. Better words will quickly lead to a better life for you and all those you influence.

DAY 1
The Power of Words

Your words have the power to bring many things, including life or death itself. Consider the power of such short phrases as "I do" or "I'm sorry" or "thank you." Those two-word combinations can change the direction of your day or the course of your life. Now consider "I can't" or "shut up" or "good-bye." Those can equally turn a conversation or a destiny.

A jury that declares "guilty" changes a person's life forever. Adding the word "not" alters it in a different direction. A stock trader's livelihood hangs on "buy" or "sell." A soldier's fate can rest on "charge" or "retreat." Words matter.

What you choose to say, both to yourself and to others, shapes the environment around you. Consider the climate you create and evaluate your words as you reflect internally and interact with others.

Words can hurt or heal. Harsh words inflict pain and provoke negative attitudes in others, like anger, fear, shame, and resentment. People can carry these words, either consciously or subconsciously, from childhood to adulthood and even to the grave. If you are careless, you may not even realize how cutting your comments can be—but others know. And here's the boomerang effect you bring on yourself: Hurt people tend to hurt people. If you are on the receiving end of verbal abuse or constant negativity, especially among those closest to you, ask whether you have had a hand in creating that environment. If you are hurting others with your words, they are likely to throw that pain back at you.

Conversely, healing words repair the damage that this life inevitably brings. By this, I don't mean fluff or platitudes. True healing words hear the heart of others, perceive their state of mind, and address them in a way that offers truth, grace, and life. Healing words hear beyond what is spoken; they speak to the soul. This takes maturity, patience, and self-control. It also requires focusing on the needs of others instead of being concerned solely with your own image, opinion, or position.

Words can destroy or redeem. How many relationships have ended because of what someone said? Employees get fired, friends walk away, and marriages end. A lie destroys trust. Gossip stirs up strife. Insults drive people away. Sticks and stones can break your bones, but words really can hurt—break hearts and start wars.

Redemptive words act as payment to regain something lost. They can compensate for mistakes, faults, and lost time. It may be owning up to something you've done, admitting you were wrong, or apologizing even when your intentions were pure. Words that seek to rebuild a burned bridge may not always be received, but they are worth the effort. Directing your speech toward construction rather than destruction pays dividends over time.

Words demonstrate either wisdom or foolishness. If you want to know what's in a person's heart and mind, just listen to his or her words for a while. What we say reflects what we think unless we consciously hide behind a mask. Most people don't—at least not for long. We eventually say what we think. When we do, we reveal whether or not we possess wisdom.

I'm always struck by the words people say when they think the world isn't listening. Whether on an open mic, a secret recording, or anonymous post . . . when the truth comes out, we find out what's really going on inside someone's head and heart. Of course, that applies to me, too. In the early days of the internet when creating anonymous or fake accounts was simple, I posted some things that revealed my own foolishness. Looking back, it forced me to examine my own heart and mind. Hidden foolishness is not smarter than public foolishness. It's actually more revealing.

Words garner either favor or scorn. How we address and respond to people creates an impression. Words that hurt, belittle, embarrass, or otherwise damage someone instill anger, distrust, alienation, and other negative feelings. Daily interaction is difficult enough without careless or unnecessary words engendering scorn. It is possible to garner favor while maintaining truth and honesty simply by choosing our words wisely.

Many years ago, I left a large company to take a job at a tech start-up. On my last day, my manager asked me into his office for my exit interview. I praised the company (genuinely) and went through the "I'm just taking a new position that I can't pass up" routine. Near the end, my manager went off script and asked something like, "Do you think I'm a good manager?" I hesitated. He noticed.

I had been to lunch with co-workers and heard them mercilessly mock him. I had watched him try to work his way up the corporate ladder, going out of his way to impress his superiors while having no idea what his subordinates thought of him. I knew the frustrations that managers of other departments had with him. I even knew firsthand that *his* manager knew of the friction around him. In truth, I thought he was a pretty good guy who was simply in over his head.

I could have done what others did (I know because they told me) and said some nice, mostly insincere words just to end the interview and move on with my life. I also could have ripped him apart, like others did behind his back. Instead, by the grace of God, I attempted tactful truth. It went something like this: "I like you. I know you know the business and have a strong work ethic.

Are you aware that many in your department and those we work with don't respect you?" (Long, awkward pause). "I'm telling you this because I hope it helps you. You either need to figure out how to gain their respect or consider going back to [your previous position] because we all know you were good at that."

He asked for my recommendations, but I admitted that I didn't know how to do his job. I had never been a middle manager in a Fortune 500 company. I reinforced that I was not trying to hurt him but help him by making him aware of the situation, even if I couldn't offer a solution. He wrapped up the interview and sent me peacefully on my way. I had no idea if he appreciated my directness or hated me for it. I wasn't even sure I did the right thing.

Months later, I ran into him at a restaurant. He was very kind. He thanked me for being honest with him in my exit interview. I asked how things were going at work, and he gave a mixed report. Some time after that, the whole department disbanded, and his managerial role was eliminated. Years later, he friended me on Facebook and consistently told me "Happy Birthday" for years. I felt I had earned his favor.

Even when telling someone something he or she doesn't want to hear, the words we use can work toward favor. Of course, some will treat us with scorn no matter what we say or do. But as much as we can control our own words, being mindful of them holds great power.

The ultimate power of our words can lead to life or death, both literally and figuratively. A false witness can condemn an innocent man to death while a message of hope can prevent someone from suicide. An abusive parent can send a child down a path of destruction while a Godly parent can instill the purpose of God in the child's life. There is no question that words hold immense power. The only question is how we will use that power.

DAY 2
Listen First

The light turned green, so I started to go. The SUV on my left didn't move. A split second later, I understood why. A car to our left was speeding through the red light. I jammed the brakes and braced for impact, but luckily hadn't rolled out too far. As the car passed in front of me, I heard a pop and scrape followed by the screech of the speeder's brakes, but felt no jarring crash. I turned my hazard lights on and got out of my car.

The other driver had stopped on the intersecting road to my right. My license plate lay in the street among pieces of the shattered plastic frame that had attached it to the front bumper of my car. I walked over and picked it up and saw the long scrape down the passenger's side of the other car. He pulled into the gas station on the corner as I returned to my car. A woman in the minivan behind me at the light stood outside her car, asking if I was all right. I held up my license plate and said, "Barely clipped me. Did you see him run the red light?"

She said she did, so I asked if she would pull over in case I needed a witness. We both pulled into the gas station parking lot, where a young man in a black suit and woman in a dark dress stood surveying the damage to their car. When I got out of my car, he yelled, "Look what you did to my car!"

Oh boy. *What I did to your car?* I thought. I wanted to scream, *You ran a red light and almost caused a terrible accident, YOU IDIOT!*

Thankfully, I didn't. He was pacing back and forth by his car while his wife stood motionless. I looked into her eyes; she was clearly shaken. No wonder, since it was her side of their car that clipped me.

"Are you okay?" I asked her, ignoring his accusation.

"Yeah," she said. "I'm sorry, we just came from his grandfather's funeral. They were close. It has been a rough day."

I looked at her husband and his anger melted to grief. "What am I gonna do?" he said to nobody in particular. "We don't have the money to fix this. I can't believe this happened."

I walked around the car to look at the damage closer. It was a nasty scrape, but to be honest, the car was in pretty bad shape already. Just another scar on an aging chunk of metal.

"It still drives?" I asked, knowing that it did.

"Yeah," he agreed.

"Fix it when you can, if you even decide to," I said. "You took my license plate off, but those plastic frames are cheap. I'll put it back on. No big deal."

He looked over at my car. There was some paint from his car on my bumper, but my car was getting old, too, so I wasn't going to worry about it.

"Just take care of your wife—and yourself," I said. "Don't run any more red lights. Things will get better."

He nodded and thanked me. I turned and went back to my car, told the would-be witness not to worry about it, and we all drove away.

I could have justified giving that reckless driver an earful, especially when he initially tried to blame me. Instead, I heard their story, asked about their wellbeing, and gave him time to cool down. Listening first turned what could have been an ugly scene into a moment of peace. It did nothing for our cars. They both had damage from the encounter that words couldn't repair, but that's where the damage ended. The more important human wreckage was avoided.

The Greek Stoic philosopher Epictetus said, "We have two ears and one mouth so that we can listen twice as much as we speak." Spouting off before listening to the facts is both shameful and foolish. Holding my tongue after the minor scrape (that was almost a major collision) kept us all out of trouble. Using my two ears before engaging my one mouth proved to be wise. Words are powerful, but sometimes silence is, too.

I wish I could say that I have always been a listener first, but it took years to learn that lesson. Even now I have to remind myself of that truth on a regular basis. "It's better to keep your mouth shut and appear stupid than open it and remove all doubt," Mark Twain famously didn't say. (It's often falsely attributed to him.) How ever that line came into being, it's often true. When we are patient enough to gather more information or hear others out before we speak, it better equips us to address things properly. Nobody wants to appear stupid, but when we speak before listening, we run the risk of doing just that. In fact, silence can make you seem intelligent, even when you aren't!

Listening before speaking never steers you wrong. It gives you an advantage, enabling you to understand others while measuring their thinking and mood. When it is time to speak, you will have a better sense of what to say. Asking questions that prod others to speak also helps to strengthen and appropriately position your response, provided you listen and hear beyond their words to perceive their heart. So take the time to pause before speaking. Give it a beat and think about what you're going to say, if anything. And make it a habit to hear others first. You'll be amazed at how much it helps you in every situation.

DAY 3
Lay Down Verbal Weapons

When I was a teenager, I had the chance to shoot a Smith & Wesson .357 magnum. In case you don't know, that's a powerful revolver with a mean kick. I found this out the hard way. Even though I had both hands on it properly, I wasn't ready for the recoil. I don't remember if I hit the target, but I remember the hammer (the part you pull down with your thumb to cock it) hit me between the eyes. The scar is faint, but it's still there!

Certain words can cut, wound, and destroy. They can be as harmful as any weapon. Like a .357, verbal weapons have a mean kick. The recoil is as likely to hurt you as much as your target. That's why it is essential that we disarm our mouths by laying down our verbal weapons.

The three most deadly verbal weapons are slander, gossip, and strife. They differ in that slander is a conscious, purposeful lie; gossip is typically unverified or truthful, yet still damaging; and strife can be completely truthful where people have honest disagreements over important issues.

Slander is the most insidious of the three since it begins with a lie and shamelessly promotes it. When I was in college, a woman in a church accused me of participating in a satanic ritual involving illegal drugs and an orgy. Sounds crazy because it was. She even accused my parents of driving me to this ritual, which was supposedly disguised as a birthday party, which they knew they had never done. It was a lie so outrageous that I thought nobody would be tempted to believe it. I was wrong.

The incident was eventually addressed in a meeting with the pastor of the church, me and my parents, the woman spreading the lie, and several church members that were involved. The craziest part was that it wasn't completely settled in that meeting. It took years for a few people to accept that she was lying and that I was totally innocent of the charges. Fortunately, truthful words stand the test of time, while lies are ultimately exposed.

Still, lies cause damage. They can ruin a political campaign, crush a promotion, cause unjust loss, destroy a relationship, and mar a reputation. And while those who promote lies may feel victorious for a time, trouble is always on the way. Shame and disgrace are waiting. A crooked heart cannot truly prosper because hatred is at the root, even though the liar may try to hide it. A lie may be the nuclear bomb to destroy all of one's enemies, but the radiation poison will eventually take its toll on the one who deploys it.

The more subtle, but equally despicable, weapon is gossip. Sure, gossip can spread lies, but most gossip involves a level of truth, though often unverified. It speculates, inflates, and disseminates negative information about people behind their backs. And it's easy to get caught up in it. Talking about people is normal, but when that talk begins to put people in a negative light, whether true or not, it's a fine line between conversation and gossip. So how do you know if something is gossip? One telltale sign is when it betrays secrets that should be guarded. Some secrets need to come to light, but others should be covered. When someone is unjustly being exposed, that's gossip.

Gossip often takes someone's wrongdoing and shouts it to the ends of the earth. But here's the difference between gossip and the rightful exposure of someone's sin: Gossip does nothing to stop it. If someone is doing wrong, talking about them behind his or her back does not stop the wrongdoing. Only confrontation has the hope of settings things right. Talking about it without taking steps to rectify the wrong is simply gossip. This kills relationships. If you want healthy relationships and a good reputation, run from gossip.

Strife is the most self-righteous weapon. When we genuinely disagree with people and use this to denigrate them, this is strife. When you are the target of strife, it is easy to respond in kind. But further strife doesn't end it; it only throws gas on the fire. Sadly, this runs rampant in Christianity. Just read the comments on YouTube or peruse a Twitter thread. Someone disagrees with a secondary view on Scripture and blasts others online, calling them heretics or false teachers. It's disgraceful. And it's even worse with political and social issues. Democrats and Republicans are at each other's throat, and social media has ripped off the mask of civility. It serves no corrective purpose and persuades no one. It just divides by causing dissension.

How do we address things we believe to be wrong while avoiding strife? Here's the trick: attack the idea, not the person. Take a hot topic like abortion. I believe it is wrong. Perhaps it's because I was the result of an unplanned, unwanted pregnancy to a young woman who gave me up for adoption because she couldn't take care of another son; or perhaps it's because I've had four children and seen a few sonograms. Suffice to say, it's a deeply personal issue with me. In my opinion, abortion becomes murder at some point. We can argue over whether that point is the moment of conception, the beginning of brain activity, the sound of a heartbeat, the point of viability, or some other time, but I do not believe that medically unnecessary abortion the day before birth is anything less than murder. Or the week before. Or even the month before. Clearly, I'm hard in the pro-life camp.

How do I address someone who supports "a woman's right to choose"? Well, it's not by calling them stupid, a sinner, or a baby killer. That just causes strife. My first question is: *Why?* Then, I listen. Getting to the motivation sets the table for a discussion that might end in a changed mind, which is the goal. Perhaps they think that a fetus is dependent, therefore not entitled to human rights. I can point out that a toddler is dependent, too. Maybe they think the fetus is not fully human until formed. Then we can talk about the stages of development. Most often, in my experience, it's compassion for the woman in a difficult circumstance, so we can talk about ways to help crisis pregnancies, then shift to the idea of compassion for the person in the womb. Sometimes it's purely political, which usually means no logic will move them. That's when it's probably best to change topics and preserve the relationship in hopes of changing the heart and opening the mind.

Bad thinking is like a cancer. It quickly spreads, but only truth will cure it. In the process, we must seek to save the patient while eliminating the illness. That means targeting ideas, not people. If you can't come up with anything that might gently bring someone to your viewpoint, it's better to remain quiet. Belittling people doesn't demonstrate your superior intelligence or moral position; it makes you a fool.

Laying down the weapon of strife can be difficult—requiring you to swallow your pride—but it's the right thing to do. The same is true with gossip and slander. Putting away all verbal weapons will not only prevent you from hurting others, but it will also keep you from doing damage to yourself.

DAY 4
Wield Wise Words

Acquiring wisdom changes the words we choose. Once we lay down verbal weapons as a destructive force, we can learn to wield wise words as constructive tools. These can be even more potent than negative language because life is more powerful than death.

Consider the four main ingredients of wise words, and imagine the possibilities when you begin putting them to work in your life.

Ingredient #1

Wise words make knowledge appealing. A man once came to my home church with a bullhorn, signs and a couple of cohorts, yelling at people as they came to the service. He was "warning of the judgment of God," accusing us of selling books, luring people in with music, and not preaching repentance. Of course, he recorded his weird display and put it online.

I admit we have great worship music. People do come because the music is really good. But how is that incurring the wrath of God? Does He prefer lousy music? As for selling books, we don't have a bookstore or book table or anything like that, so he was completely making that part up. But even if we did, who cares? Books benefit people! But he really tipped his empty hand by accusing my pastor of not preaching repentance. He does. Routinely. Obviously, Mr. Bullhorn had never stepped inside our church.

But let's pretend he did have a point about something. By standing at the edge of our church property screaming distorted accusations, he did nothing to sway anyone's mind. He just looked like a nutcase. Any knowledge he might have had would be lost in the wind. He made what he had to say extremely unappealing. That's not wise.

Ingredient #2

Wise words are persuasive. One slightly funny moment in the protest video was when a church attendee looked quizzically at the small group for a moment, then asked, "Who are you protesting?" The bullhorn guy kept ranting, yelling random and unrelated things. The church attendee shook his head in confusion and walked away.

This incident is an extreme example of foolishness, but it clearly demonstrates the ineffectiveness of words with zero persuasive power. The protester's words were loud but completely wasted. He had no intention of listening to anyone. Truth didn't matter; only his display did. If he had a legitimate complaint, he would enter the church, get to know the staff, then choose fewer and gentler words to penetrate the hearts and minds of people. Bullying and manipulation don't have a lasting effect. Wise words lead people to think, reflect, and willingly change.

Many things can get in the way of wise words. An antagonistic tone will be heard louder than any truth spoken. Belittling words and phrases can detract from the real point. A public rebuke can be unnecessarily humiliating while a private reproach may be better received. And a self-serving showcase, like Mr. Bullhorn, will convince people that it's not about a message for others, but about the self-righteous person with the camera pointed at him. Though there will always be some who reject wisdom and knowledge, we can be people who make truth appealing and persuasive so that more hearts and minds will be won for God's Kingdom.

Ingredient #3

Wise words come when you know your audience; this is the most important rule of communication. Netflix thinks I want to watch the new season of *Gilmore Girls*. In truth, I'd rather drink toilet water. They recommend this revived teen-girl series because my daughter watched it from my account several years ago. Now when I go to catch a police drama like *Bosch* or *Jack Taylor*, it doesn't know the difference between me and my daughter, so it hits me with ridiculous suggestions. This is a classic case of not knowing your audience.

On social media, I often see Christians arguing with non-believers about politicized topics by quoting the Bible. Many of these people completely reject the Bible, so the good seed falls on hard ground and dies. They will, however, often respond to things like logic and science. This requires a knowledge of various things and a level of critical thinking; but for those who reject the authority of Scripture, there are still powerful, persuasive arguments to be made. After all, the same God who inspired the Bible created the human mind and the natural world. If they seem at odds with His Word, it's only because there is an error in human thinking.

Before you can influence someone's thinking, you have to know who you are talking to. This requires patience, discernment, and most importantly, listening. Before sounding off with your opinion, learn to probe the thinking of the person or persons to whom you are speaking. Learn where they are coming from so you can better walk next to them to lead them to truth, rather than lining up in opposition and forcing them to play defense. Knowing your audience requires caring about your audience, which always puts you in a position to better empathize and communicate.

Ingredient #4

Wise words are nourishing. That means they feed the soul. We all know people whose words drain us, leaving us parched and exhausted. Christians are not to be these people. Instead, we should speak words that pierce the natural to bring supernatural nourishment. The Hebrew verb we translate *nourish* or *encourage* literally means "to pasture, tend, graze, or feed." It's the same word used in the 23rd Psalm: "The Lord is my shepherd." A more literal translation of that phrase is "God *tends* to me."

These are the kinds of words we must learn to speak. Our language must feed the souls of those we encounter. They must give life. They shouldn't wear people out; they should make them want more. Of course, there will always be those who do not have "ears to hear," but we don't measure the wisdom of our words by whether someone receives them. We measure them by the standard of Scripture and inspiration of the Holy Spirit. Those words, when received, will bring people closer to God and help them look more like Christ.

Creating a habit of wielding wise words makes us more effective as we make God more attractive to people. Learning to address people where they are at and in a language that they understand forms a more fitting reply. With a little practice, you can master the art of delivering a timely word. And that's a beautiful thing!

DAY 5
Don't Give Offense

Some people will be offended no matter what you do or say. Even so, it is well within our power to communicate in such a way that strives to avoid offense. This goes beyond the obvious, like name-calling and insults. The type of offense that I want to consider here is the kind that causes someone to stumble morally.

Consider a few hypothetical, yet common, situations:

- A nice-looking man or woman walks by in a restaurant while you're having lunch with a friend. You make a salacious comment that causes your companion to turn and look. That look turns into lust.
- A co-worker who is a bit of a jerk proposes an idea that is not very good. Instead of politely countering it or dismissing it, you lay out all the reasons why it's the dumbest thing ever suggested, knowing it will embarrass and denigrate him.
- A friend is having a hard time with her marriage and relays an incident that upset her. You respond that you always knew her husband was a dirtbag, and he's never going to change.

- Someone tweets something mean at you. You rip into them, shocking people that know you. The whole world can read it.

Congratulations, you've just given offense! Invoking anger, jealousy, lust, resentment, despair, and other morally destructive feelings plants a seed of destruction within one's soul. When our words or actions are designed to transport someone to a worse place, we expose the worst within ourselves while stabbing at the worst within them. This is an offense given not by circumstance or necessity, but by choice. Human nature grabs hold of this type of offense, so it's our responsibility to refrain from handing it to people.

In the same way, giving offense in the name of "honesty" is no excuse. Honesty is not intentionally cruel; however, preceding it with "I'm not gonna lie . . ." or "I don't mean to be offensive, but . . ." does not excuse the pile of excrement you're about to dump in someone's lap. Wrapping it in the guise of truth does not make it any less offensive. If anything, it makes it worse. If the truth is going to lead someone to a destructive place, virtue demands you hold that truth inside.

Avoiding offense also means awareness. Sometimes seemingly innocuous things can trigger a person's downfall. When you are aware of it, you bear some responsibility for it.

After graduating from college, I used to gather with some college friends and, being poor, we would play poker for a five-dollar buy-in. It was cheaper than a movie or meal. We'd play all night with a nickel ante and quarter maximum bet. One night four of us had gathered, and the host said that a mutual friend whom we hadn't seen in a while would be joining us.

"We can get a good card game," I suggested.

"Not tonight," the host said. He told me that our friend had developed a gambling problem and was seeking help for it. Playing cards would be terribly irresponsible, even though the money was insignificant. The last thing he needed was a bunch of his friends engaging him in something that would remind him of his struggle. We gladly did other things that night. Knowing his compulsion, we were responsible for the offense it might have given.

You can't go through life without offending someone, but you can make the decision to avoid it whenever possible. Trust me: You don't want to be known as an agent of offense, especially to those you care about. Winning back an offended friend can be harder than taking over a city. Considering the impact of your words and actions will enable you to be more sensitive to the direction you are leading people. Take them to a healthier, more positive place, and you will have more peace, more happiness, and more friends.

DAY 6
Don't Take Offense

Fyodor Dostoyevsky wrote in *The Brothers Karamazov*:

> "A man who lies to himself is often the first to take offense. It sometimes feels very good to take offense, doesn't it? And surely he knows that no one has offended him, and that he himself has invented the offense and told lies just for the beauty of it, that he has exaggerated for the sake of effect, that he has picked on a word and made a mountain out of a pea—he knows all of that, and still he is the first to take offense, he likes feeling offended, it gives him great pleasure, and thus he reaches the point of real hostility."

Dostoyevsky wrote that in 1880, but it sounds even more true today. We live in an age of anger. Almost everyone is offended by something, and they wear it like a badge of honor. People are offended by politicians, traditional marriage, minimum wage, the national anthem, the names of sports teams, old white men, the weather, and just about everything else. It's as if you're not moral unless you're morally outraged. Being offended is *en vogue*. You're not cool if you're not ticked off.

Such willingness to be offended is merely self-righteous indignation. It has gotten completely out of control. At the Claremont

Colleges near Los Angeles, white girls were told not to wear "winged eyeliner, lined lips, and big hoop earrings" because they "belong to the black and brown folks who created the culture."[1]

Outside the courthouse in Seattle, human urine and excrement cover the sidewalk, yet Councilmember Larry Gossett opposed power-washing the sidewalks because it brought back images of hoses used against civil rights activists.[2]

In England, the National Union of Students was instructed to stop "clapping and whooping" at their annual conference because it excluded deaf people. Instead, they were encouraged to use "jazz hands." (Never mind that inaudible expressions exclude blind people.)

When Georgia Governor Brian Kemp signed a bill banning abortions if a fetal heartbeat could be detected, Disney, Netflix, and Warner Media were so offended that they threatened to pull all production out of the state. Never mind that Disney had recently shot movies in the United Arab Emirates and Jordan, Netflix continued production in Egypt and Jordan, and Warner Media worked extensively in Northern Ireland and collaborated with the China Movie Channel. All of these countries had much more restrictive abortion laws than Georgia proposed.[3] Apparently, being offended requires selective taste.

While it's true that offense will come your way, here's the catch: *You don't have to take it with you.* Offense is a two-part transaction: one gives, another takes. Just refuse to take it. You will feel better for it, and the giver will be left holding their own nastiness.

The dangers of living in a continuous state of offense are numerous. Short-tempered people do foolish things. They are quick to engage in a fight, both verbally and physically. Their anger gets them in trouble again and again. Deep down, they are miserable. Don't let their misery stick to you. Be wise and stay calm when insulted. Deflect anger with a gentle response. Maintain an even temper. Don't give that type of person the satisfaction of getting to you. It will usually irritate people even more when you *don't* get offended, but let's stick to the altruistic motive and rise above it because it's the right thing to do.

That's not to say that some things are not offensive. They are— or at least, they should be. Slavery was a terrible offense. Perhaps because not enough people found it offensive, it went on (and still goes on) for too long. Racism continues to be an offense. But the proper response is not more racism. The only way to rid legitimate offenses is with a better response. In the case of racism, we should practice and promote respect for everyone while building bridges across the chasms that divide us. Simply expressing anger over an offense does nothing to solve it.

The first time I went to Mozambique and saw children dying of starvation, I was offended by the abject poverty. It didn't just make me sad; it made me angry. There was no glory in their suffering—no purpose in their pain. A long line of human corruption created conditions where the weakest and youngest paid the most dearly. My sense of injustice, however, turned from anger into action. I've spent most of my life working for an organization that now provides emergency food for over 350,000 children every month. And though I still find abject poverty to be an offense against humanity, I don't carry it with me in a personal, unhealthy way. In other words, when someone leaves food on their plate at a restaurant, I don't scream at them about their insensitivity or privilege. Nobody likes being lectured by someone with a chip on their shoulder. You'll also find yourself dining alone if you do that.

Learn the difference between petty offenses that need to be ignored and serious ones that need to be defeated. That's the difference between taking it *in* and taking it *on*. Dealing with real offenses in a constructive way means moving beyond the emotion to find an action that helps others. So choose your offenses wisely, taking on the ones you can do something about and leaving behind the rest.

DAY 7
Don't Toot Your Own Horn

Comedian Brian Regan has a great bit about people who always talk about themselves, savoring the moment when they can impress others with their life story and achievements. He makes fun of those who listen blithely to others tell their stories, then jump in to turn the attention to themselves and their superior tales. The bit is called the "Me Monster."

"What is it about the human condition that people get something out of that?" he asks. The obvious answers are insecurity, egotism, or competitiveness. But it may go even deeper than that.

A 2012 Harvard study used brain imaging to discover that sharing information about oneself triggered the brain similar to eating food or having sex.[4] Yeah, it's that serious. We are hardwired to talk about ourselves and show off. Most of us are born with an inner "me monster" eagerly waiting for the right moment to jump out.

Social media just stokes that fire. Facebook connects us so we can keep up with each other. Instagram puts our lives in pictures. Twitter allows us to express our thoughts in shorthand. All of these can be helpful, but they can also push us to present the best of us. The result can be self-aggrandizing and narcissistic. Like any tool, social media can be useful or dangerous. When the "me monster" runs rampant online, it magnifies the ugly side of self-promotion.

UPGRADE
Your Words

How do we maintain a healthy balance? It's not like we shouldn't ever talk about ourselves or post a vacation photo or celebrate an accomplishment. What is too much? Here's a simple rule of thumb: Let others praise you; don't do it yourself.

Parenting can make it even worse because our children can serve as extensions of ourselves. Bragging publicly about a child's accomplishments may seem like a nice confidence booster for the child, but it can also appear showy. Always consider the other parents and children seeing or hearing it. Are they truly interested in celebrating with you, or does it make them feel inferior because their children are not as successful? We have to maintain a healthy balance between supportive and braggadocious.

It can also be as innocuous as insensitivity or unawareness. This is where I've stumbled into trouble. Conversation turns to something of interest to me and in my excitement to share, I one-up someone else or talk too much about myself. It's humbling (and a little humiliating) to have that pointed out, but hearing it made me more conscientious of what I say, when I say it, and to whom I'm speaking.

Self-awareness is the key. Hear your words, and notice how they are received by others. Don't demand an audience or push for a place among the "in" crowd. It's better to wait for others to build you up than to be disgraced as arrogant or self-centered. Remember what Brian Regan says and bury the "me monster."

WEEK 3

"Being busy does not always mean real work. The object of all work is production or accomplishment and to either of these ends there must be forethought, system, planning, intelligence, and honest purpose, as well as perspiration."

—THOMAS EDISON

UPGRADE

Your Business

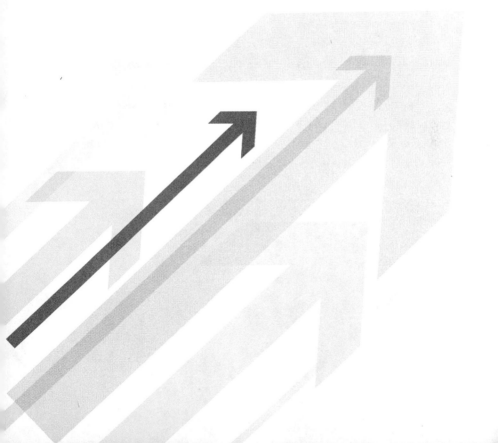

We all have to make money. But it's important that we don't let money make us. Chasing money means missing life. When what we do defines who we are, we've lost our identity.

The balance between the necessary pursuit of wealth and the higher calling of who we are created to be lies in our attitude toward work and money. Material things make lousy gods. If they don't abandon us, we eventually abandon them when they throw dirt on our coffins and lower us into the ground. On the other hand, work can create essential character in us, teaching us valuable lessons that transcend our bank accounts.

Putting business into the proper perspective enables us to succeed financially while utilizing the rewards for things that last for generations. The right attitude toward work allows us to benefit from our labor without being a slave to the almighty dollar.

DAY 1
Get off Your Butt

The first thing you need to know about work is that it is necessary. The earth contains an abundance of wealth, and mankind was designed to tend to it. As we have moved away from an agricultural economy, it can be hard to see; but consider how even modern technologies are derived from the earth. Silicon, which powers our phones and laptops, is sand. Next to oxygen, it's the most abundant element on the face of the earth. The third most abundant element is aluminum, which can be found in everything from flat-screen TVs to space rockets. Yet all of these things would still be in the ground if people hadn't worked to figure out how to use them in amazing ways.

There is something inherently good in creating value through work. In the story of creation, God worked, observed His creation, and declared, "It is good." Mankind, created in the image of God, has a built-in sense that creating something through hard work satisfies a need. Even something as simple as mowing the lawn or vacuuming the floor brings a sense of satisfaction, accomplishment, and self-worth.

It is proper to take pride in our work when we do it to create something good rather than to receive praise from others. If others notice it, and even acknowledge it, that's fine. But the right kind of pride in one's work performs the same with an audience as it does when nobody is looking. When it's done right, we know it's done right. We can say, "It is good," and be content with that. There's no need to brag about it.

Work doesn't always garner a check. For most of her life, my wife has never received a paycheck, but she has worked very hard. Taking care of a home and raising four children is not a 40-hour workweek; it's 24/7. She has held far more job titles than I have. She has served as a cook, cleaner, driver, counselor, teacher, nurse, interior decorator, and a few more professions. The "pay" was zero, but the benefits were immeasurable.

Refusing to work, however, is destructive—not only to oneself but to society as a whole. Laziness leads to poverty. It robs you while you sleep. Thinking about it won't do it. Talk is worse than cheap; it's flat broke. Profit only comes by getting up and getting it done.

There's a strange movement for "guaranteed income," even for people who don't work. Being physically unable to work is one thing. Welfare as charity to help those unable to function is not a right, but a generosity. A healthy society will care for those in such need. But being picky or just plain lazy doesn't deserve a paycheck. It is good for workers to have an appetite; an empty stomach drives them on. If you refuse to work, you literally don't deserve to eat.

I took my family to Curaçao for vacation one year. This amazing desert island sits off the coast of Venezuela and is part of the Dutch Antilles. The rugged beauty of the mountains and cliffs is enhanced by the pristine coral beaches and plentiful sea life. It's a nature lover's paradise.

We stayed in a house on the west end of the island, away from the town, where the best dive sites lay. Nearby was a cliff known as a prime spot for jumping into the ocean. Let me tell you, it is high! Though the water is plenty deep, it's also crystal clear. You can see the white, sandy bottom from above. Of course, we had to check it out, so one day my older son and I swam over to it from our beach. There's another beach close to it, so we got out of the water and took some stairs up the side of the cliff and skirted an outdoor café to get in position. It was a little terrifying, but we both took the plunge.

My other children wanted to see it, so a few days later we were driving to another beach and decided to stop. From the road, I had a hard time finding it. I passed it a couple of times before realizing that the café was obscured by what looked like a junkyard. We parked the van and followed the path through rusty chairs, overgrown pots, and an old refrigerator, among other things. Inside the café, it wasn't much tidier. In fact, it was downright ratty. The owners sat inside while a couple of people took their lunch on the patio outside. Other than the incredible view, I have no idea why anyone would eat there. I'd be more afraid to eat the food than jump off the cliff.

Those in my family who dared, took the leap, then we dried off and continued to our destination, but I left thinking, "How could such potential be so wasted? Tourists would flock to that place if they would just clean it up!" It's like they were sitting on a gold mine but never collected on it because they were just plain lazy. A little effort would go a long way.

Charles Spurgeon said, "The sin of doing nothing is about the biggest of all sins, for it involves most of the others." Work is necessary and good. Without it, we miss the reward it brings. We never know the gold mine we are sitting on until we put some sweat into it. Even the most menial work improves our lives and the lives of others.

No matter what you have been taught or what you may believe, there is one thing you absolutely must get into your head: Work is good. It is necessary, honorable, and essential to your wellbeing. So get up, go out, and find some work to do.

DAY 2
Work Hard

Ralph Braun was a young boy when he was diagnosed with spinal muscular atrophy. Within a few years, he was unable to walk. Rather than give in to the crippling effects of the disease, he put his time and energy into engineering the first battery-powered scooter. Through his determination and hard work, he could now get around unassisted. Still not satisfied, his next step toward independence was to modify a postal Jeep with what became the world's first wheelchair lift.

He began to notice that others could benefit from his inventions, so he started building more on weekends and in the hours after his full-time job at a factory. People drove from all over the country to have him modify their vehicles. His personal drive and hard work led to the founding of Save-A-Step Manufacturing in 1963, which grew into The Braun Corporation in 1972. Near the end of his life, he started The Ralph Braun Foundation for those in need of mobility equipment. In 2012, he was a recipient of President Obama's "Champion of Change" award.

When he passed away in 2013 at the age of 72, his company stood as the global leader in mobility products, surpassing $200 million in sales.[5] It continues today, all because of the hard work of a young boy who refused to let his own disability limit him.

Once we take the first step and get out to do some work, we have another choice: work enough or work hard. This is one of the keys to real success. Though it might not start with a high-paying job, this is where a high-paying job begins. In fact, the low-paying job is often the test to see if we deserve promotion and reward. Those who work hard when others are working just enough don't stay in the same position; they move on and move up.

Here's a truth—proven time and time again—for every person who feels like his or her job does not matter, is unimportant, or lacks personal fulfillment: When you work hard at a job you don't like, you put yourself in a position to get the job you want. When companies promote from within, they typically look to see who performs the best in a lower job in order to move him or her up. Countless CEOs have risen through the ranks. If your job has a ceiling, you will know when you have hit it and possess the confidence to step into another company with ease and experience.

Hard workers become leaders. Leadership is not handed out randomly; it's earned. Any successful leader will tell you that hard work is one of the most important qualities required to succeed, if not the most important. Michelangelo said, "If people knew how hard I had to work to gain my mastery, it would not seem so wonderful at all." President Theodore Roosevelt said, "Nothing worth having comes easy." Thomas Edison said, "There is no substitute for hard work." All of these men knew firsthand that greatness in any area can only be achieved through hard work.

It is possible to have a job and still be lazy. If you've been in the workforce for long, you've probably seen it. There's a saying: "Lazy people don't even cook the game they catch." This speaks to those who do the job halfway. This frustrates everyone around them. They are as irritating as someone blowing smoke in your face. If something is worth doing, it's worth doing fully and completely.

A friend got a managerial job in a warehouse of a large international company. He had spent decades working hard on his own, but came to the point that he needed the stability and benefits this corporation offered. After a few months on the job, he realized something that shocked him. If something needed to be moved from a loading dock to the other side of the warehouse and five items could be loaded on a cart and easily pushed to its destination, the workers would just load each item one at a time. When he questioned them, they gave him an excuse related to union regulations or some other nonsense. He discovered that they would take their time for two primary reasons: first, they were not hard workers, and second, it gave them the opportunity for overtime, which meant time-and-a-half pay. He could not believe it. In his mind, if you are working, you work hard. When the job is done, you rest or play. Instead, he found a bunch of people who worked, but were still lazy. They worked just enough to call it work.

Hard work also benefits us in areas of life not related to our occupation. It forces personal development and growth, solving problems and overcoming challenges wherever we find them. This applies to marriage, parenting, volunteering, and even recreation. The payoff comes in the form of better relationships, more enjoyable experiences, and the satisfaction of contributing something of value in everything we do.

Our work ethic also serves as an example to others. A spouse appreciates the effort we put into the relationship. Children learn to emulate our work habits. Reliable co-workers notice and follow our lead. Quality friends are drawn to someone who takes pride in his or her work. Our reputation is built less on what we do than how we do it. Respect is gained in every area when we work hard to fulfill a task with excellence.

Talent alone is not enough to really succeed. There are plenty of talented people. The one thing that separates them is the work they put into developing their God-given gifts. In 2009, Ralph Braun wrote, "I had two strikes against me. I was young, and I was what the population calls disabled. I never let that stand in my way. I just had to walk the extra mile, or roll the extra mile in my case."

That extra mile separates working enough from working hard. And that makes all the difference.

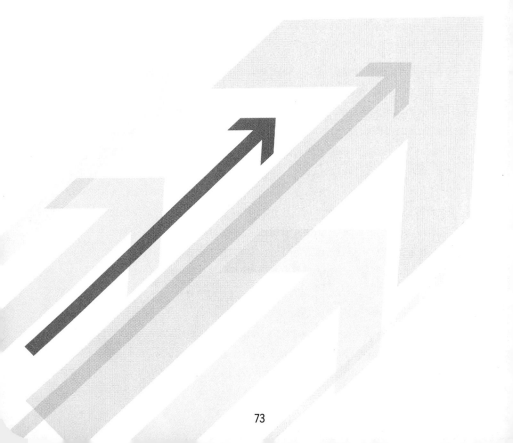

DAY 3
Work Smart

Thomas Edison is regarded as the greatest American inventor, if not the greatest inventor of modern times. His work on telegraph- and telephone-related products, the phonograph, the electric light bulb, motion pictures, the electric generator, fuel cell technology, and the lesser-known, but commercially successful, cement products and processes revolutionized life at the turn of the 20th century. By the end of his life, he had 1,093 patents to his name.

However, his first invention, though successful in form, failed in the marketplace. At the age of 22, Edison filed for his first patent for the electrographic vote-recorder, a machine designed to accelerate and improve the legislative process by electronically recording and tabulating voice votes. He took it to the U.S. Congress, where it was resoundingly rejected. Faster votes meant less time for filibusters and political dealing. Politicians were not interested in efficiency, so Edison's hard work and innovation bombed. From that early lesson, Edison determined that he would focus his efforts only on things that would succeed not only in form, but also in the marketplace.

In addition to working hard, it's important to learn how to work smart. An old saying captures the importance of knowing how to apply hard work: "He who gathers crops in summer is a prudent son, but he who sleeps during harvest is a disgraceful son." In agriculture, there is a season for certain work. One must be smart enough to know when to plant and when to harvest. Working hard on the wrong thing in the wrong season does not pay off, but working hard and working smart lead to bounty.

The same principle applies in all areas. In Edison's case, the season wasn't right for an electrographic vote-recorder. Today, you just have to turn on C-SPAN during a vote to see the electronic tally on the screen. Edison was several decades ahead of his time.

In the early days of internet-delivered television, a Christian television station developed an IP-based delivery system with their own box along the lines of Roku and AppleTV. The problem was that most Christian television consumers were older, less technologically adept, and used to watching Christian programs over the air or on cable. The venture, though on the cutting edge of technology, failed. It was a nice idea, but not a smart one.

Perhaps the greatest example of "not smart" in our era is the story of Blockbuster Video. In the age of video cassettes and DVDs, Blockbuster ruled the movie rental space. Thousands of stores served millions of customers. In 2000, the founder of an upstart company flew to Blockbuster headquarters in Dallas to propose a partnership. The idea was that this new company would run Blockbuster's brand online, and the stores would promote this new online service in its stores. The proposal was laughed out of the room. The entrepreneur was Reed Hastings, the founder of Netflix.

A few years later, Blockbuster tried to replicate the Netflix model while leveraging their massive storefront presence, but it was too late. People had moved on. The board fired their CEO and reversed course, returning to the things that had made them profitable—and obsolete. By 2010, the once-dominant company was bankrupt. A decade later, Netflix topped 150 million subscribers worldwide, with revenue approaching $20 billion a year.

Of course, for every successful tech start-up, there are a hundred flops. Particularly ugly are those get-rich-quick schemes. While they are not new in principle—people have been peddling such things for centuries—the internet made it easy. Though some ideas may work for a short time, wealth from get-rich-quick schemes quickly disappears. Wealth gained through smart, hard work grows over time. Chasing fast, easy money is simply not smart. A person who chases fantasies has no sense.

Finally, working smart means knowing when to take a break. Don't wear yourself out trying to get rich. Be wise enough to know when to quit. Stories abound of successful people working ridiculous hours for years. While their achievements may be admirable, there comes a cost. No amount of success is worth sacrificing family, healthy friendships, and rest.

Jimmy Johnson coached the Dallas Cowboys in back-to-back Superbowl wins in 1993 and 1994. At the time, he was consumed with winning in the NFL. One week before his first championship, the *Deseret News* ran an article about him that reported, "Once he became coach of the Dallas Cowboys he calculated that he would have no time for marriage. So he divorced his wife, Linda Kay, the college sweetheart he married in 1963."[6]

He essentially traded his wedding ring for a shot at a Superbowl ring. That's not smart; it's sad. Obviously, the marriage didn't mean much to him at the time. "I just wanted to live alone," Johnson was reported to have said. Football had already separated him from his life partner and the mother of his children. Though he is rightly admired in the world of sports, the model he set for success is not one that should be followed.

Even God took a break from work. After six days creating the universe, which is no small task, He took a day of rest. Of course, God doesn't get tired. He didn't need a nap. Instead, He was setting the example for mankind, essentially giving us a day off. It's not about what we do on that day, but rather what we don't do. One day out of the week, we don't do what we do for labor. Taking a break from work is healthy, beneficial, and wise. It makes our workdays more productive and keeps us from burning out.

Not knowing when to quit is not the mark of success. Working smart allows for time away from a career. Learn the prudent way to get things done, work hard at it, and make time for other important things in life.

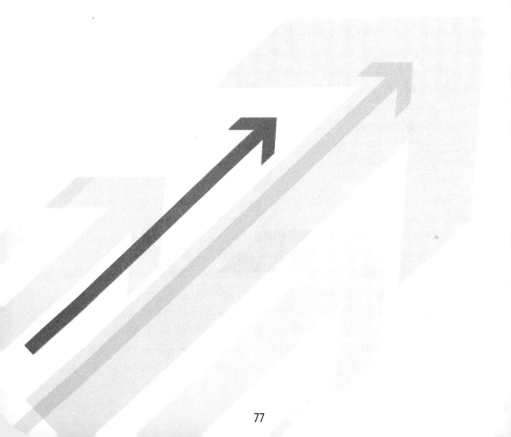

DAY 4
Gain Things the Right Way

Ever since the end of the Great Depression, Americans have been brainwashed. Thanks to a carefully crafted advertising campaign and a tightly controlled market, young men have been willing to part with an average of two months of wages for a small rock as a precondition to getting married.

"A diamond is forever," the DeBeers Mining Company told us. Though huge diamond resources had been discovered in the 1870s, the South African company owned 90 percent of it and needed a way to create value. Several decades later, the marketing campaign took hold. By 1940, the diamond ring became the only way to show true love—and it wasn't cheap.[7]

In the late 90s, the world woke up to the fact that the multi-billion-dollar diamond trade was financing violence, primarily in Africa. These "blood diamonds" brought millions of dollars to warring factions in countries like Angola and Sierra Leone. Children were often forced to mine them, while armed militias poured the profit into civil war. To their credit, DeBeers and other leading diamond companies took action through what's known as the Kimberley Process, attempting to verify the source of the diamonds and prevent them from fueling blood conflicts. Still, the protocols did very little to stop the poorest of African countries like the Central African Republic, Zimbabwe, and Congo, from exploiting workers (many of them children) in the mines. The head of a regional mine in one of these countries summed it up by saying, "We have so much wealth, yet we stay so poor."[8]

Diamonds pass through so many hands from mine to market that it can be extremely difficult to trace and regulate, but one thing is certain: Many people have profited from ill-gotten gain. I know when my wife and I got engaged, we never thought about where the diamond in the ring I gave her came from. As far as I was concerned, it came from the jewelry store. Sure, it cost way too much, but it was so ingrained in our culture that a proposal demanded a diamond that I didn't have the awareness to even question it.

Today, even with the ability to "grow" flawless diamonds in a lab, the marketing forces remain strong, insisting that only "natural" diamonds are legitimate. There are many conscientious diamond miners in countries like Canada and Australia, but the price and demand are still at such levels that abuse remains in other parts of the world. Children still forego an education in order to slave long hours sifting in muddy waters for a sliver of stone that will put food on the table.

The diamond industry is not the only place where ill-gotten gain takes place, of course. Examples can be found from Wall Street to Main Street. Wherever someone can cheat, exploit, or steal, human nature tends toward corruption. But it's better to be poor and honest than to be dishonest and a fool, because the wealth that evil brings has an even higher price. The wages of the righteous is life, but the earnings of the wicked are sin and death.

Misery accompanies theft, lies, and abuse. Expensive cars, nice clothes, and ornate mansions cannot mask the spiritual rot demanded by such tactics. "Stolen bread tastes sweet, but it turns to gravel in the mouth" (Proverbs 20:17 NLT). Those benefiting by ill-gotten gain often don't realize this biblical truth in the moment.

Their deception includes self-deception. Some understand it late in life, seeing clearer in hindsight. Regardless, the truth of the matter does not change.

Wealth itself is not the problem; it's the means by which it is gained. Hard work and smart work must be accompanied by honest work for it to be meaningful and rewarding. Looks can be deceiving. Don't assume that wealth, or lack of it, measures one's character. A person should never be judged by their pocketbook. The account that matters most does not hold cash; it holds currency that cannot be traded in the marketplace.

If you treat people right, you will find the kind of success that money can't buy. It may result in great wealth or simply provide for your basic needs, but it will always pay dividends in peace, friendships, integrity, and honor. You can always sleep well at night and walk with your head up every day when you know your income is untainted.

DAY 5
Be Frugal

As a freshman, my daughter lived in a dorm and dined on campus. In the first week, she and some new friends found the big plastic cereal dispensers at breakfast one morning. One was labeled "Lucky Charms," and my daughter filled her bowl with some. As they ate, she commented to another girl, "These are just like Marshmallow Mateys!" Her new college friend looked at her like she was from another planet. That's the moment my daughter discovered that she had been raised on the off brands.

With my wife working at home to raise our four children (all within six years of each other), bulk off-brand items were a regular thing. Frugality was a practice we learned because it was the only option. Clothes were handed down. School lunches were packed, not bought. Vacations were determined by cost (Got a place we can stay free? We'll be there!) For a while, we had one vehicle—a used minivan. When I took a job that required driving downtown every day, I picked up an $800 Ford Escort with no air-conditioning. Summer was brutal, but it put me in a position to eventually get a better car.

Thankfully, those lean times didn't last too long, but frugality never left. I still mow my own yard (though I plan to give that up one day). I change the brake pads myself on the cars. The carpet upstairs is over 20 years old (that will go soon, I hope). My wife enjoys shopping at those stores that sell last year's name-brand clothes at a greatly reduced price. We still cut coupons. I know how to work airline and hotel points to the max.

It's not that we're cheap; it's just that when something can be obtained for less, why pay more? I'm not opposed to nice things. If you can afford the top-of-the-line of everything, go for it. Rich people are great. They buy things, which provides jobs. They donate to the arts, churches, children's hospitals, and all sorts of life-enriching things. It's just that I'm not one of them. So if there's a way to get it done for less, I'm going to figure out how to do it.

Even when spending money on luxuries, you can be frugal. Airbnb has changed the way I vacation. Netflix has replaced the movie theater. Streaming music services saved me from my CD-buying addiction. I still go on vacation, watch movies, and listen to music. It just doesn't cost me much.

Being frugal is all about avoiding unnecessary expenditures while getting the best value for your money. Just because you can afford something doesn't mean you should buy it. This extends beyond personal habits to business as well. Technology has made it possible to communicate for far less than in the past. Going paperless, using teleconferencing instead of travel, networking through social media, and outsourcing can all be utilized to cut costs while achieving the necessary outcome.

Working for a non-profit organization, I'm very conscientious of "business" expenses. If I'm attending a conference, I stay down the street at a hotel half the price of the one hosting the event. I'll hit a grocery store in town and buy snacks I can carry with me rather than buy a $15 burger at the convention hall. I fly coach. I can look donors in the eye and assure them that I am maximizing their gifts.

Of course, there is a balance. Frugal is not stingy. Workers should be paid a fair wage. Servers should be tipped appropriately.

It's really about knowing what is worth the expense and what is waste. And it's especially about rejecting a life of pursuing pleasure in material things. You don't always have to have the best, latest, and most impressive.

Ironically, this is a path to wealth, because you don't blow through cash as soon as you get it and you get the most out of each dollar. Learn to love frugality, and you will be wiser with whatever you have.

DAY 6
Stay out of Debt

Full confession: Frugality is easy for me. Staying out of debt? Much more difficult. As soon as I seem to get ahead financially, something comes up. A car breaks down. Someone gets sick and racks up medical bills. An expense comes out of left field and catches me off guard. Let's just say that I have enough experience with debt to say that it's far better to stay out of it!

Proverbs 22:7 says, "The borrower is servant to the lender" (NIV). In today's society, the "lender" is not typically a person. It's a bank or credit card. Banks can be tough rulers, but credit cards are downright tyrants. They promise freedom, then throw you in prison. I'm convinced that if there weren't laws against it, they would take your children as payment. Their power over you should be removed as fast as possible.

Many helpful books and videos exist to provide detailed steps to avoiding debt, but the bottom line is this: Create a budget, live below your means, and build your savings.

I've lived without a written budget. That's like carrying water in a bucket with holes. Things are spilling all over the place, and your bucket is constantly empty, but you're not sure why. Once you write down what you're spending, you start to see the holes. Once you see them, plug them. And here's a tip I learned the hard way: Don't budget according to your paycheck. In other words, don't assume you can spend what you earn. Stuff happens, and it's the stuff that sends you backwards.

People smarter than me say to budget 50/20/30. Fifty percent should be allocated for basic needs, including housing, utilities, transportation, healthcare, insurance, and groceries. Twenty percent should be set aside for savings and existing debt, like school loans. The remaining 30 percent can be used for giving to church or charity, dining out, vacations, and luxuries—like that new laptop or TV subscriptions.

Living below your means requires you to stick within the budget. New cars are great, but they aren't a good value. One that's a little used, like 20,000 miles or so, has already depreciated the steepest, so you're getting more for your money. I recommend driving it into the ground, which is why 150,000 miles isn't an unusual odometer reading for me; but as long as you're not driving yourself into debt, do what makes you comfortable.

Trust me. Spending more than you have leads to chasing more income, which enslaves you to finances. It's a miserable place to be. Unexpected expenses have cost me weekends and evenings that would have been better spent with my family. In hindsight, better planning would have served me well.

Staying out of debt also means learning the "tricks of the trade." Don't let the government take more in taxes than legally required. (Don't cheat—they'll catch up with you.) When taking out a loan for a car or house, ask questions. Banks know the numbers, and they know how to take advantage of them; so dig, push, and get the best deal you can. Personally, I take advantage of zero finance deals. Those are great as long as you stay disciplined and pay them off in time.

Negotiate the heck out of everything. I needed a car for my son and had a budget, so when I found one I wanted, I told the dealer that I would pay a certain amount and no more. He countered. I left my phone number and told him to call me if anything changed. For the next week, he called almost every day, lowering the price each day, but still above what I offered. Eventually, he caved, but even if he hadn't, I was patient enough to keep shopping until I found one within my budget. I have also been (over) charged thousands of dollars for emergency healthcare but paid a much more reasonable rate by playing hardball. Patience is a big part of staying out of debt.

Do whatever it takes to stay out of debt. Delay that purchase or vacation. Shop and compare rates. Fight when it's appropriate. Repair things yourself when you can. Cook your own meals. Borrow when you need something for a short time. Don't compare yourself to anyone or try to keep up with others. Debt is a jerk, so don't give it room to rule.

DAY 7
Master Ambition

Ambition is energy that has the potential to work for us or against us. When properly channeled, like electricity, it empowers us to work hard and smart. When unleashed without restraint, like lightning, it can destroy. Most people want to achieve something positive and that's a good thing, but when that drive becomes overdrive and ambition consumes us, the consequences can be devastating.

Unrestrained ambition can make us monsters. If you haven't seen it by now, you will run into it soon. It could be on a sports team at school—that person who wants to win so bad that he or she abuses everyone else on the team in the quest for victory. Even worse, it could manifest in an individual desire to be the star, tearing down teammates in the process.

At work, it shows up in the person climbing the ladder as fast as possible, with you as another rung to be grabbed, stepped on, and left behind. I've seen it in creative settings, where people are supposed to collaborate on a project, but no ideas are as good as those of that overly zealous genius.

At home, a parent can place too much pressure on a child to succeed, whether in athletics, academics, or other areas. Even worse, a parent can live vicariously through a child, projecting his or her ambitions onto a son or daughter. Hang around sports teams long enough and you will eventually encounter a dad who treats a recreational league like a tryout for the pros, pushing a son or daughter to achieve the father's failed athletic ambitions.

That's the kind of ambition we must avoid like a deadly virus. Remember the response to COVID-19? People wore masks, maintained distance, cleaned surfaces, and avoided touching things. Ambition needs an equally conscientious response. We need to guard our words, stay away from the negative aspects of it, scrub our hearts and minds, and avoid temptation. Deadly ambition is prevalent in our world. It's even contagious. But we actually have more control over it than we do a virus. Here are a few warning signs for ambition that have mutated into something vicious and nasty.

Ambition that feels threatened by the strength of others.

Some people fancy themselves as leaders or the smartest person in the room. The difference between a real leader (and a truly smart person) is that a good leader knows how to develop others, recognizing, cultivating, and guiding their gifts and talents. Negative ambition rarely notices people's strengths, only their weaknesses. If it does spot strength in another, it views it as a threat to be neutralized. It can show up as racism, sexism, and other forms of bigotry. Or it can belittle, berate, and betray someone to maintain dominance. This is particularly sad because healthy aspirations will recognize potential in another, gravitate to it, develop it, reward it, and make a stronger team.

Humility is the grease that keeps the ambition engine from overheating. When it's gone, people get burned. After that, the engine freezes up or blows up. Looking for ways to help others succeed and grow is a better path to our own success. This keeps us focused outwardly, sensitive to the needs and interests of others, and humble. Then we can begin to see the uniqueness and abilities of others as something to celebrate, not subjugate.

Ambition that makes us prisoners.

If unchecked, our desire to achieve can overtake and enslave us. While under control, it makes a good servant, but if it becomes the master, it is cruel. The feeling that "it's never enough" is a curse. Even if you're the best in one area, there's always someone better in another. Plus, a feeling of discontentment robs us of thankfulness, which is a key to happiness.

The thing about prisoners is that they always end up alone. If you become subservient to your ambition, you'll drive all your real friends away. It may even cost you your family. They say it's lonely at the top and the ones who say that are usually the ones whose ambition crushed everyone around them. Subsequently, they are left in a self-constructed cell perched high atop whatever mountain they sought to conquer. Sure, we can all see them way up there at the pinnacle of their world, but appearances can be deceiving. The penthouse cell is still a prison cell.

Ambition that makes us miserable.

The great irony of a controlling drive to be "on top" is that the end game—whether money, position, power, or fame—never brings the expected happiness. That's why many rich, powerful, and famous people are miserable. Don't get me wrong: A person can be all of those things and be fulfilled, but it's because the wealth, position, or notoriety comes as a byproduct of meaningful purpose. People who pursue wealth because they love money, power, or fame are never satisfied. Those who pursue excellence, purpose, and meaning and gain wealth or recognition for it are better positioned to enjoy it and use it to help others.

True prosperity is found in a content soul. Ambition is not the path to happiness. It is frequently more often the obstacle, although it doesn't have to be. It doesn't matter whether one is rich or poor, known or obscure, president or peon. The relationship between ambition and happiness is the same for everyone.

Fulfillment comes from finding purpose, not chasing an illusion. When we find our place, there is real joy.

Ambition that makes us a god.

By "a god," I mean the supreme being in our lives, the center of our universe, the one who decides right from wrong, and the one we serve before all others. This narcissistic state is marked by self-centeredness, self-absorption, self-promotion, and selfishness. All of our focus, efforts, thoughts, and goals bow down to the Great Self.

This path points in the exact opposite direction of all that is worth pursuing. When we choose to honor the real God with the best of everything we produce, then we find an abundance of everything that is good. Trading a life in pursuit of God for seating ourselves on His throne is the height of arrogance and foolishness. Our ambition must be directed by a power higher than ourselves, and the ultimate power is the One who created the universe and everything in it. He walked the earth as a man, gave His life to bridge the gap between Himself and mankind, and invites us to follow Him to forgo the pain of misguided ambition for finding peace, contentment, joy, purpose, and fulfillment in His grand design for our lives. That sacred ambition will never confine us; it brings true freedom.

Master your ambition by putting it in third place. Put God first and other people second. Then your energy will be harnessed so that it operates under control, enabling you to power the success of everyone around you without subjecting them to death by electrocution.

WEEK 4

"Show me your friends and
I will tell you what you are."

—SPANISH PROVERB

UPGRADE
Your Friends

Do our friends make us, or do we choose our friends according to who we are? Good question, and one that could be argued either way. One thing is clear: Our friends reveal much about our judgment and character.

Attending grade school presents an odd scenario. We grow up with classmates and neighbors, naturally gravitating toward certain other children out of the necessity to form bonds. As we grow up, most of those friends fall away. The older we get, the more our friends result from our own choosing, rather than situational necessity.

The more we intentionally choose our friendships, the more meaningful these relationships can be—if we choose wisely. We need friends, even outside of marriage. They can provide encouragement, companionship, and accountability. Conversely, they can also become burdensome, distracting, or destructive. So it's critical that we understand how to form constructive bonds as we choose our friends.

DAY 1
Choose Your Friends Well

A Harvard Medical School study tied meaningful relationships to health, happiness, and longevity.[9] I'm guessing that they only studied *good* friendships, not bad ones. It doesn't take long to realize that lousy friends can drain you of all joy and suck the life right out of you.

There are many attributes in people that make them good, quality friends; but I want to focus on three in particular that are at the top of the list: the wise, the even-tempered, and the reliable.

The Wise Friend

You probably know by now that foolish friends can get you in trouble. They tend to be full of bad ideas. Following their lead takes you places you later regret. But did you know that you can become a wiser person by hanging around wise people?

A wise friend can be worth following, imitating, and learning from. If you watch closely, you will see if that friend's life is producing the qualities you need, like peace, joy, kindness, and goodness. That means looking beyond the career, possessions, and outward appearance. When you get close to someone, you see what's really going on in his or her life. If it's real, it's worth finding out the habits, ideas, and actions that led to the admirable outcome. It's also worth learning the mistakes that friend may have made and learned from so that you can avoid making them yourself. A truly wise friend can help guide your way to happiness and fulfillment.

The Even-Tempered Friend

Avoid hot-headed, angry people. They can poison your mind and drive you to say and do things that cause unimaginable harm in your life. The trouble they stir up will spill onto you at some point. If you have a friend exhibiting bitterness, anger, and a foul temper, there is an easy way to figure out whether you should try to help that person work things out or back away and leave God to deal with them. Point out his or her anger. If they admit it, apologize for it, or ask for help, then you have a good chance to walk them out of the darkness. Try to be that guiding light. However, if they respond in denial or, not unexpectedly, more anger, then you should probably draw the line there. If you feel it's appropriate, leave the door open for future relationship, but let them know that you need distance from their anger. Do not let allow them to have control over you, either by negative influence or intimidation.

It may be painful to enforce distance from a friend or loved one, but given that they can also drive away other beneficial friends who see you associating with them, you may find that you replace one negative relationship with a dozen positive ones. Someone with an even temper will serve as a stabilizing force in your own life. The one who is not easily annoyed is far less annoying—and not nearly as dangerous. There is enough in this world to agitate us. A friend who calms the soul is a friend worth seeking and keeping.

The Reliable Friend

Finally, when a friend proves to be unreliable, keep your distance. Trying to maintain that friendship has been compared to chewing with a broken tooth or walking on a twisted foot. It can be difficult and even painful. As much as you should strive to be a reliable friend, you'll be better served with someone who returns that reliability. A friend in need is a friend indeed, but when you're in need, is that friend there for you? Quality relationships work both ways, friends helping each other, sticking together through the good times and the bad. If you can't count on someone, don't count that person as a close friend.

There's a difference between being friendly with people and being friends with them. Everyone should be treated with kindness, honored as one created by God. But we should only bring in a select group of people as close friends. Not only is it permissible to be choosy with our friends, it's necessary.

DAY 2
Forget Fools

A fool is someone who lacks good judgment or common sense. You can give them the best advice in the world, and they will ignore it. I once had a college friend who was easy-going, good-natured, and adventurous. He had a great sense of humor, which I thoroughly enjoyed. Generally, my kind of friend.

But soon, he started exhibiting signs of bad judgment. It showed up first with his words, then his actions. He was from another state, so for spring break we drove halfway across the country to visit his family. As we planned our mini-vacation, he suggested some things that made me uncomfortable. Things I knew were wrong. I blew off his talk because we were teenagers, which meant we said a lot of dumb things. When we arrived at his house, his parents welcomed me. His father was a pastor, and my friend talked a good game around his family. I figured his foolish talk was just that—talk.

That night, we went to visit a friend of his. That's when they started smoking something that was definitely illegal. Turned out the only phony talk was what had taken place around his parents. I politely refused to participate in their illicit activity. The next morning, I got up before he was awake, packed my car, and drove a few hours to stay with another college friend. I figured he could find his own way back to school.

He made it back, but the friendship was over. I wasn't rude, I just quit hanging out with him. I made my share of mistakes in college (no illegal substances!), but his foolishness sent me running away from him. I have no idea where he is now or how he's doing. I wish him well, but our brief friendship is long forgotten.

We all have lapses in judgment. We all make mistakes. The difference is the pattern. Is foolishness the exception or the rule? Are lapses in judgment recognized as mistakes or defended as "no big deal" or "me doing my thing" or "my truth"?

True friends impart wise counsel. They help steer you in the right direction with sound thinking and proven values. They don't always tell you what you want to hear, but what you need to hear. They may even confront you or challenge your decisions, but it will always be with your best interest at heart.

That's not something you will get from a fool. Their reasoning is not to be admired, emulated, or followed. Most of what they tell you should go in one ear and out the other.

There's a great illustration in nature. Nothing is more terrifying while swimming in the ocean than the sight of a shark fin headed your way. But it could just be a curious or playful dolphin. The most obvious difference between the two is in the shape of the dorsal fin, but that can be hard to distinguish when you are out in the water with them. Another thing to look for is the motion of it. The tail fin of a dolphin is positioned horizontally, meaning it goes up and down to propel it through the water. A shark's is vertical, so it goes side to side. You likely won't see the tail above water, but the motion means the dolphin's dorsal fin usually bobs up and down, disappearing and reappearing. A shark's fin won't do that. If it's swimming near the surface and heading for you, the fin will be consistent. That's when you panic.

We can all be like dolphins, curious in nature and sporadically bobbing between smart decisions and dumb ones. That's where wise friends help keep us on course. Sharks are dangerous because they are consistently foolish. They won't heed good advice. Wise counsel is wasted breath. They may even despise your advice. That's when you panic.

The reason for keeping a safe distance from fools is not to make yourself feel superior, protect your image, prove your righteousness, or anything like that. I'm not suggesting you cut every one of them off completely, just that you limit how close you bring them in. You should continue giving good advice but refrain from confiding in them. It is not necessary to eliminate your influence on them but critical to mitigate their influence on you. Recognize that they are not someone in whom you place your trust. They are acquaintances not friends. And when one turns out to be a dangerous shark, get out of the water.

DAY 3
Don't Compare

A hamster wheel is designed for exercise, but watching a hamster running on one while going nowhere is pretty funny. I suppose they are just the rodent version of treadmills, but they still make me laugh.

My son once had an exercise wheel for a pet hedgehog. That was a nightmare . . . literally, a *night*mare. Hedgehogs are nocturnal, so that chubby guy was spinning that wheel throughout night, which quickly gets old when you're trying to sleep. To make the annoying seriously disgusting, the hedgehog would defecate while running. Yes, he'd poop in his exercise wheel, churning it round and round.

I graciously give you this vivid mental picture because when we begin comparing ourselves to others—our possessions, our status, our achievements, our number of followers—we voluntarily step into that rodent wheel. It never ends, and it never gets us anywhere. It just wears us out. Even worse, if we start acting out in response to these comparisons, we're filling our spinning cylinder with what amounts to excrement. Not only do we begin to look ridiculous to everyone who sees what's going on, but it stinks to have all that filth flinging around.

Here are three truths about comparisons to help you stay out of that nasty, tiresome place:

First, only you are you. That means you are not anyone else (in case that isn't obvious). When you compare yourself negatively to someone else, you are judging yourself by what you perceive to be a standard of success that he or she has attained. You probably don't know the whole story of that person—the failures, the hard work, the sacrifices—and you've baselessly assigned a standard to yourself that is not realistic. You don't need to be as rich as the wealthiest person you know. You don't need to be as attractive as the most beautiful person you know. You don't need as many followers as the most popular person you know. You just need to be who you were created to be.

Conversely, comparing yourself to others and judging yourself to be better also creates a false impression. The "thank God I'm not like them" standard is pretty low these days. Just watch reality TV. There is always someone a little lower on the chart. Falling into this trap can create an undue sense of accomplishment. Just because you are better off than someone else doesn't mean you are reaching your full potential. Don't get lazy or complacent by comparing yourself to someone worse off than you.

Second, contentment brings peace. When you are happy with yourself, even while working to improve yourself according to your own worthwhile goals, then you can rest well at night. You don't need to spin the wheel endlessly. The envy that inevitably comes with comparisons will rob you of all peace and joy. Be happy for the success of others and find your own success. You may be a good mother or father, you may enjoy a job that improves the lives of others, or be an encouragement to people wherever you go. Do what you're supposed to do, and let others do their thing. When you seek to do what's right instead of what makes you feel like you're keeping up with others, you'll find that you are more secure, more complete, and much more content.

Finally, success can lead to pride. If you measure yourself by others and find that you measure up, you'll probably attribute that success to your own doing. Even if it's true, that sense of self-made success will very likely cause you to take pride in your achievements; but pride always precedes destruction. When you compare yourself to others and strive to equal or beat them at whatever game you're playing, you're going to want to gloat when you win. However, if you will simply focus on your own goals, without constantly comparing yourself to everyone else, then your achievements will lead to a healthy sense of satisfaction, independent of everyone else. This will enable you to enjoy your own success while acknowledging and appreciating the success of others. Seeing the success of others without being jealous of it keeps pride away.

The endless wheel of comparison gets you nowhere. Run your own race, keeping your own pace. When it comes to having better friends and being a better friend, this is key. If you're always comparing and competing, you're not a friend, you're an opponent. To go with a sports analogy (a nice break from the hedgehog wheel image), it's better to be a teammate than a constant adversary. That means helping others in their success and letting them bask in glory at times. You don't have to be the one in the endzone every time, or the one shooting the puck or scoring the goal. Sometimes an assist is better. Nobody likes a "ball hog." If you're the lineman on a football team, nobody expects you to score a touchdown. They expect you to block so someone else can score. Measure yourself by the task in front of you, not by the accolades of others.

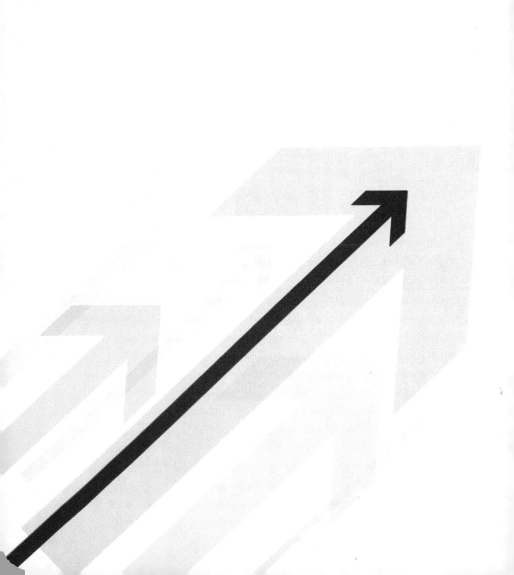

DAY 4
Don't Chase the Crowd

There's an easy temptation as we live, work, and play in this world. That's to go along with the crowd in order to gain acceptance or assume that something is true because it's a view held by the majority. The problem is that crowds aren't always right. Historically, they are often wrong. Following them can lead to some bad places.

A major issue in our country, and even the world, is the topic of "climate change." When I was growing up, the scare was global cooling, then it shifted to global warming. Now it's just climate change. Apparently, science changes as fast as the weather. Without getting into the whole debate as to whether man is causing catastrophic conditions, or whether it's within our power to stop a coming environmental apocalypse, I want to focus on one aspect that accompanies this debate: the issue of "scientific consensus."

Any time the climate change debate comes up, proponents almost always cite "scientific consensus." This means that every scientist agrees with the overall idea. The problem is that they don't, which logically means that scientists who don't agree ("deniers," they are called, as if denying a theory is somehow inherently evil) either aren't scientists or they don't get a voice. I strongly suspect it's the latter. But here's the thing that gets me, and the whole reason I bring up this touchy issue: Christians who believe in climate change often cite scientific consensus, too. As if because scientists say it's so, then it's so—the same group of scientists who largely agree that God does not exist.

Science cannot prove (or disprove) that a God-man was killed on a cross and came back from the dead, not to mention the miracles listed in the Gospels. Why? Because science limits itself, by necessity, to the natural—things in nature that can be tested and re-tested to give the same result every time. God is decidedly *not* natural; He is beyond nature, or supernatural. God is outside the scope of popular science. Yet Christians cite "scientific consensus" on future predictions as if the case is closed.

Here's the truth: Scientists could be 100 percent right about climate change, and scientific consensus would still be an insufficient reason to believe it. Consider a few other matters of "consensus" in the past.

Charles Darwin's 1844 scientific treatise (published in 1859) is still considered the foundation of evolutionary biology. Its original title was *On the Origin of Species by Means of Natural Selection of the Preservation of Favoured Races in the Struggle for Life.* Yep, "favoured races." Meaning, of course, white people. As his own views evolved, he was very direct. The "Negro" and "Australian" (referring to aborigines) were considered much closer to gorillas than "the Caucasian." Killing them was a matter of "natural selection."[10] Scientists still hold Darwin in high esteem despite this blatant racism.

Up until the 1960s, scientists agreed that the topography of the earth—mountains, valleys, continents—was created when the earth was very hot, then cooled. The center of the earth, they thought and taught, was solid. Alfred Wegener, a German meteorologist and son of a preacher, noticed that the continents fit together like a puzzle. He came up with the idea of a single super-continent called Pangea that floated on a molten core, allowing movement and explaining earthquakes, volcanoes, and such.[11] His theories were not taken seriously. Twenty years later, this was taught in all science classes.

In 1985, the *New York Times* cited "broad scientific consensus" that acid rain was destroying lakes and forests and threatening people's health. Six years later, at the end of a $500 million study, it was determined that "acid rain was not damaging forests, did not hurt crops, and caused no measurable health problems." Seems acid rain did more damage to budgets than anything else.

Even within the climate change camp, major shifts have taken place. Al Gore's financial backing of palm oil as an environmentally friendly biofuel crashed spectacularly.[12] Now massive clearing of land to grow palm oil is being blamed for accelerating damage to the environment. Oops.

Most recently, the world literally shut down its economies because of COVID-19. A prime catalyst for this reaction—causing massive job loss, financial insecurity, and psychological damage we still haven't seen the end of—was a study done by Imperial College in London. It predicted that the United States alone would suffer 2.2 million deaths if no measures were taken. If we did the things we did in the "lockdown," we would only see 1.2 million deaths. Extreme measures to save a million lives seemed the right thing to do. Fortunately, we only witnessed a fraction of that. While every death is painful, the overall pain of the nation was nowhere near what was predicted. I call that a huge "win," but it also points to something else: the imperfection of science.

Despite the past and present failures of the scientific community, I'm not down on science. The word *science* is literally derived from the Latin for "know." Knowledge is good. Science is a continuous learning process which is rarely conclusive. It's okay for scientists to be wrong. What is *not* okay is for us to blindly follow the crowd that cries "scientific consensus!"

Pressure to follow a popular idea can be dangerous. Friends that ostracize you for not going along with the crowd are not good friends. If they can't convince you with sound thinking, they will usually resort to bullying and petty insults. Those are the type of people to avoid. Don't even waste any time considering it; just turn away from them and keep moving. Don't envy their status with those in the spotlight or desire the approval of the majority. They will only stir up trouble.

True friends accept you even when you don't agree with them. They will respect your ideas, even while confronting and challenging them. This is, of course, a two-way street. If you want to be a good friend, you must treat others with respect even while chipping away at ideas you believe are wrong.

Remember, when we disagree with others, the goal should always be changing their mind for the better, not tearing down their character. Sticking to your principles is only as good as your principles. When you are convinced that an idea is right, it is incumbent on you to persuade others, when possible, to see the rightness of it. When you realize you are wrong about something, change your mind. It is simple and demands no shame. Heck, scientists do it all the time, and they are hailed as deities in secular society. As a human, you are inevitably wrong about something. There is some idea or belief deep down in your brain that is just plain wrong. When you figure out what that is, gladly cast it aside. The fewer of those you hold, the better off you are. Be glad when you rid yourself of a wrong thought. Just make sure you form your ideas of right and wrong, good and bad, just and unjust, acceptable and unacceptable from what is true, not from what is popular.

DAY 5
Be Loyal

Perhaps the best compliment one can give a friend is that he or she is loyal. In the context of friendship, loyalty simply means consistently being a friend. It doesn't mean approving of everything someone does, agreeing with them all the time, or even spending much time with them. It means that when someone needs friendship, you offer it.

Loyalty requires kindness. It offers a hand in a time of need. When it's necessary to distance yourself from someone because that person is behaving in a way that is destructive, it means refraining from being a part of that destruction. Honesty demands that we tell the truth to friends, even when it's something they don't want to hear, but loyalty balances that with a glowing neon sign that says, "Open 24/7." Values are not compromised when we speak truthfully, yet lovingly. On the contrary, truth balanced with openness proves the principle that our friendship is loyal.

It doesn't even demand that friends clean themselves up before coming to us. The offer to bring their lives to us, messy and broken, with a guaranteed response of unconditional love (not to be confused with unbound acceptance of their beliefs and actions) demonstrates the strength of our commitment as a loyal friend.

That's not to say that loyalty doesn't have boundaries. It does.

Loyalty does not suffer abuse or allow another to take advantage of you. Instead, it holds securely to righteous values with one hand while extending an open hand to others. Picture a person reaching over a cliff to help another. He or she holds tight to a rope or rail while reaching out with the other hand to pull someone away from the precipice. This is loyalty. The very nature of its immovability provides the promise of security and safety that others need.

Another important aspect is confidentiality. This, of course, has limits. If someone is committing a crime or being put in danger by another, then loyalty demands that you stop the situation from getting worse, but those situations are not typical. When someone confides in you, there is an expectation that their concern, problem, pending decision, or other issue be held between friends. The absolute worst thing you can do is share their confidential matters with others. People talk. Gossip spreads like a cold at daycare. Breaching a friend's trust is a lightning-fast way to ruin the friendship and incur wrath or resentment.

Loyal friends are also supportive. They get in the thick of things with each other. A phrase popped up many years ago that irritated the language student in me, but was pretty good at communicating an idea. People started saying, "Let's do life together." My literal mind initially reacted with, "Do life? We live life, embrace life, celebrate life, struggle through life . . . we don't *do* life!" Eventually, I got it. It was all of those things, just not alone. Doing life together means spending time together, maybe over lunch or coffee, talking about the big things and the little things, making connections with other people to form a community, and supporting each other through the good times and the bad. It means celebrating with others in their triumphs and crying with them in their pain.

The traditional value of individualism—taking care of yourself and your own—encourages responsibility, initiative, and self-determination. But without community, it's naked and vulnerable. We need the support of others, and we need to support them. Healthy connections are not dependent relationships in the sense that we are helpless on our own, but they are constructive as we hold each other up. It may require sacrifice at times, but it always returns dividends. We are not solitary creatures. We need each other.

Finally, loyalty breeds loyalty. If you want friends, be friendly. If you want loyalty, be loyal. That doesn't mean you won't get burned from time to time, but when others burn bridges, it cuts you off from future trouble. If we build enough bridges, the better ones will be left standing. Naturally, this requires you to be the bridge-builder and not the bridge-burner. That's why faithfully practicing loyalty only works on a consistent basis over time. It's like planting a garden. You throw out more seeds than you plan to see grow, knowing some will take and some will wither. If you plant one or two seeds, the best you'll get is a plant or two. But when you sow generously and then cultivate your investment, you are guaranteed a harvest.

Sow loyalty. Cultivate it with kindness, honesty, trust, and support. You'll be a better friend and reap better friends.

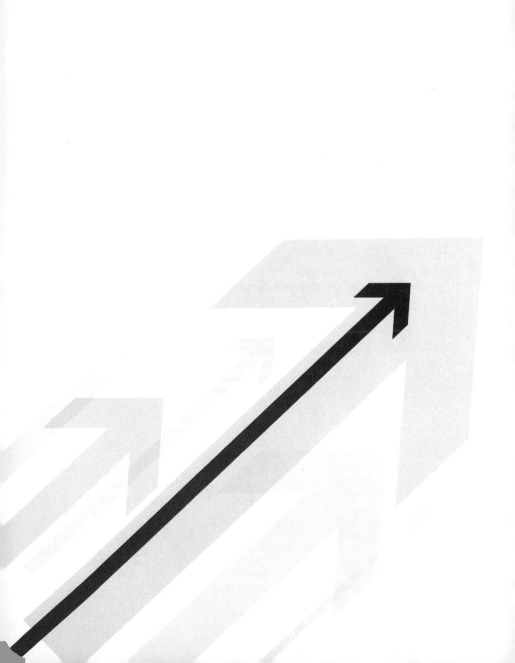

DAY 6
Make Peace

Making peace means more than simply avoiding conflict. There is a balance between avoiding toxic people and running from every uncomfortable situation. While it may be necessary to remove or restrict certain relationships to maintain peace, it is often necessary to work through conflict and disagreement to find real peace. There are several proactive mindsets you can adopt that will foster peace in you and in your relationships.

First, approach people with love. If you are consumed with anger, resentment, or hatred, you will find yourself living in a constant state of conflict, both internally and externally. Negative thoughts have a way of making their way from your brain to your mouth. Those words fill the atmosphere like negatively charged ions in a storm. Eventually someone will be struck by your lightning, sparking division and strife. Your friends, if they have any sense, will distance themselves from you.

When we emanate love, joy, laughter, and encouragement, it attracts the right kind of people. In fact, if others are full of negativity, their opposite polarity will push them away. You will simultaneously draw healthy relationships your way while creating a natural separation from those who will likely cause trouble.

Love may not work with some people. They may even resent or

abuse your love. But even in the worst situations, love will never fail you. When others receive and respond to love, it works. And when they expose themselves by rejecting love, it enables you to see the truth and move on. The result is that you either make peace between the two of you, or you walk away with your own peace still intact, knowing that you maintained an attitude of love.

Next, practice forgiveness. Was your love rejected? Let it go. I know it's easier said than done, but when you carry the pain inflicted by another, waiting for reconciliation, retribution, or other resolution that never comes, you don't punish the person who caused the real or perceived pain. Instead, you hurt yourself.

People will do you wrong; that's a given. Forgiveness lets go of the hurt others cause, but it's more for your benefit than theirs. Dwelling on the pain does more damage to you than it does the person who caused the pain. And when you've been hurt, you're more apt to hurt others. That cycle of pain creates a whirlwind of destruction all around you. Whoever hurt you ends up destroying you and damaging those around you. Frankly, they don't deserve that kind of power.

Unforgiveness is by far one of the most toxic emotions you can harbor. Imagine that slight, insult, betrayal, or other harm as a hot coal. The longer you hold on to it, the more it burns you. Release your grip on it. Refuse to squeeze it in your soul where it simmers, sears, and scars. I don't actually like the phrase "forgive and forget." That begs for repeated abuse. Instead, forgive, learn, set it aside, and move on. This allows peace to calm your soul once again, which, in turn, allows peace to permeate your other relationships.

Finally, look for ways to put the needs of others above your own. On the surface, this may not seem connected to personal peace, but it can, when properly practiced, lead to a level of gratitude and contentment that nurture an inner peace.

I have experienced this many times while visiting the relief programs I've been involved with for years. Not too long ago, I spent a week in Angola, Africa, where we camped out in tents for three nights in a remote area. By remote, I mean no electricity, no water, no nothing. That also means no toilets, which, for me, is kind of a big deal. To put it bluntly, I don't like relieving myself in the woods, especially in the sparse vegetation of southwest Africa. I can deal with the "shower tent," which is a bucket of water and a tall, slender tent that blows in the wind. I can handle a cot, brushing my teeth with bottled water, hearing wild animals during the night, having sand in my shoes, and all of that. But the toilet thing is a bit of a deal breaker. But I wasn't there for me. We were there to document the difference between villages without our emergency feeding program and those that have it. In some, we saw lethargic, malnourished children spending every day looking for a meal. We even witnessed a funeral. In the others—the ones where we're providing food—we saw healthy, laughing children going to school. Huge difference. Way more important than my toilet anxiety. By focusing on the needs of others, I had peace. Even while squatting in the woods. Wild animals, insects, and all.

You don't need to go to Angola to find real need. It's already in your city, county, or neighborhood. It may even be in your own house. Be the answer to someone else's problem, and you'll find your own problems diminish in importance. When your problems fade, peace prevails.

One word of caution: Helping others in need doesn't mean making their problems your own. This applies more to emotional and psychological difficulties, which are easier to take on than physical ones. For example, if you're helping people through depression, don't take on their depression. A good doctor is not one who catches your illness, but one who helps heal you of it. That means finding the level of need you can alleviate while maintaining your own health. Don't get in over your head. Just look for opportunities where you find joy in helping others and do what you can. Peace will follow.

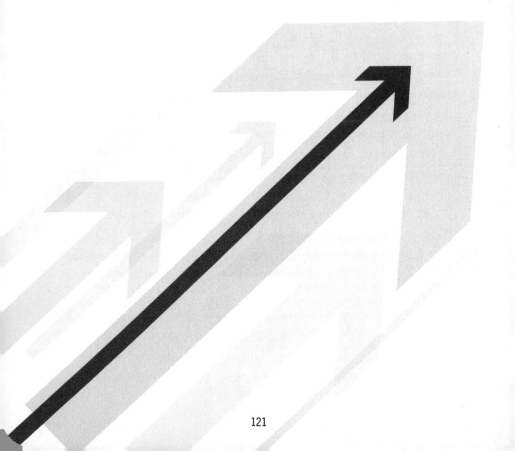

DAY 7
Poach on Enemy Territory

Everybody seems to have a little German in them. We often take pleasure from the misfortune of others—an emotion called *schadenfreude*. The literal translation is "harm joy." An innocuous form would be laughing when someone trips and falls. A few seconds on social media reveals a more malicious enjoyment when something bad happens to someone well known. As a society, we love it when our enemies suffer.

Scripture warns against this. "Don't rejoice when your enemies fall; don't be happy when they stumble" (Proverbs 24:17 NLT). In Jesus' great Sermon on the Mount, He instructed His followers to "love your enemies and pray for those who persecute you, so that you may be sons of your Father who is in heaven" (Matthew 5:44 NASB). By taking it a step further, He didn't simply tell us to not hate our enemies but to actually love them. This, He says, is requisite to calling God our Father.

How do we do this? Proverbs offers a concrete plan: "If your enemies are hungry, give them food to eat. If they are thirsty, give them water to drink" (Proverbs 25:21 NLT). In Luke's account of Jesus' sermon he records Him as saying, ". . . do good to those who hate you, bless those who curse you, pray for those who are abusive to you" (Luke 6:27b-28 NASB).

This is not easy. It does not come naturally to us. Doing it out of obedience is praiseworthy, but consider another possibility. Maybe you can turn an enemy into a friend. Maybe by exercising God's principles, you can poach on enemy territory, change someone's life, and claim a friend for yourself.

Years ago, I was in a group with one particularly opinionated man—let's call him Lee. He didn't just express his thoughts openly and loudly, Lee stated them with an aggression. Foolishly, I took the bait a few times and challenged him. This did not produce thoughtful dialogue or energetic debate; it drew his wrath. Soon, Lee began going out of his way to irritate me. He mocked me in front of the group, which really bothered me. He even threatened to punch me in the face on one occasion.

I didn't want to get out of this group, so I swallowed my pride and implemented a strategic approach to win him over. I quit challenging him since this clearly pushed his buttons. I chose my words around him much more carefully. When things leveled off between us, I started asking his opinion on things he was interested in, which he enjoyed expressing. I took a genuine interest in his views. I asked him to help me in simple ways that were easy for him to do, then thanked him. When he celebrated something in his life, I celebrated with him. When he was hurting, I showed empathy. Eventually, he became a friend. Now when I see him, neither of us bristle. We greet each other with sincere warmth.

Lee and I are not getting each other's names tattooed on our chests any time soon. It's not like we're that close, but we are on good terms. We can be alone with each other and have a good time. If he needed me, I'd gladly be there for him. I'm pretty sure he'd be there for me too. The point is that there are times when it is within our power to turn a bad situation into a good one. We can transfer some names on our enemies list to our friends list. When we master this art, we work on a whole different level.

Think about those people you dislike the most, and ask your-self if any of them are candidates for friendship. Go out of your way to do something good for them, fulfill a need, or say a prayer. They won't all respond like Lee did, but the odds are in your favor; and God is on your side when you are kind to those who treat you poorly. You just might upgrade your friends by convert-ing an enemy.

WEEK 5

"...you can't give up on your family,
no matter how tempting they make it."

—RICK RIORDAN, *THE SEA OF MONSTERS*

UPGRADE
Your Family

You choose your friends, but you're stuck with your family. At least it feels that way at times. But having strong family relationships is a key to stability, security, and happiness. Of all the areas outside of yourself, family has the most potential to make your life better or make it worse. Why wouldn't you do everything within your power to make it better?

Perhaps you have a great family. If so, count your blessings. The steps in this chapter will be easy, and they will bring you even greater joy. The icing on that cake is that they will also bring more happiness to your family. For many, family can be a bit difficult. Maybe even miserable. If that's the case, then these may be some of the most important words you read.

The reality is that whatever your family situation is like, these truths can help you, even if there's nothing that can help your familial relationships. If your situation is less than perfect, it may take a long time to see results with your family members, but you can immediately feel better about yourself, knowing that you are doing the right thing.

DAY 1
Honor Your Parents

"Honor your father and mother . . ." It's one of the Ten Commandments, so it must be important, right? If you're hating this section already, hang on—there's hope. But let's start with the basic idea: honor. What exactly does that mean? Most people think, *show respect.* That's only partially right. The more literal meaning of the word used by God in the Old Testament means "to make heavy" or "to give weight."

The dynamics of this change over time. As children, we are under their authority. Barring abuse, criminal activity, and other extreme circumstances, children should obey their parents. If you're a child struggling with whether or not you should obey your parents, I'd recommend talking to a few respected adults, like pastors or counselors, and working through your issues.

Once you're an adult, things change. You're no longer bound to obedience, but you're still bound to honor. The authority of parents ends, but the duty to honor continues. How do we "give weight" to our parents, whether we are children or adults? Here are some basic steps.

First, take their legitimate needs seriously. Keyword: *legitimate.* It requires wisdom, discernment, and maturity on your part to know the difference. Again, this shifts over time. As a child, your parents provide your basic needs, so a little appreciation and cooperation gives them the respect they deserve. As an adult, most parents need to feel valued even though they are less integral to your family. Keeping the proper relationship can be a balancing act and will vary as widely as our individual personalities, but a decent rule is to allow parents as much of a role as they want as long as it doesn't interfere with your wellbeing and, if you're married, the wellbeing of your spouse and children. The older our parents get, the more the basic needs come into play—things like food, shelter, and medical care. Elderly parents often need assistance, and nothing is more heartbreaking than one whose family doesn't seem to care. If your parents are seniors, take the time to ensure that their basic needs are provided. Take them to the doctor if they need a ride, or at least make arrangements if you cannot do it yourself. Pick up the phone and call. The small things make a big difference. They won't be around forever, so honor them in their legitimate needs while you can.

If you're in the difficult position of having really rotten parents, focus on that keyword *legitimate*. To illustrate this, allow me to paint the worst picture I can imagine. To me, the worst scenario I can conjure is the father who sexually abuses his daughter. If you want to bring the mother into it, I'd consider the one who ignores or enables the exploitation an equally horrible parent. Now consider the legitimate need in this situation. It's not to protect, accommodate, or even obey the parents. The biggest need in this situation is for the abuse to stop. Immediately. And at all costs. In this nightmare situation, the child needs to expose the abuse. That means telling people in authority, including the police. The father legitimately needs to go to jail. If the victim is a minor, the mother needs to lose custody of the child. Yes, this will bring shame to them, but they need to be shamed. In fact, their only path to redemption requires that they be held accountable for the abuse. If you're in this situation or another where the parents are doing wrong, know that it is 100 percent honorable to stop the wrongdoing by any legal means necessary.

Second, listen to them. If you're a teenager who thinks your parents know absolutely nothing, keep listening. You'll be shocked to hear some good advice from time to time. They've been around longer than you and seen a few things, so don't shut them completely out. If you're an adult, keep listening to your parents, even if only out of courtesy. Be patient and hear them out. Above all, be nice. Respect their role in your life even if you don't respect everything they say or do. Pursue peace with them, even if it's not always achieved.

Third, live a good life. This is perhaps the highest honor we can bring to our parents. If you marry, marry well and love your spouse. Work hard and provide for yourself and loved ones. Raise your children right. Fight through every problem and never give up. Be light in a dark world. Even if your parents never recognize it, your right living brings them honor. After they pass from this life, your good life and the goodness you pass on brings honor to their names.

Finally, pray for your parents. Whether they are beloved saints or complete monsters, you can pray for them. Whatever their need—health, finances, purpose, change—you can ask God to intervene in their lives. Never underestimate the power of prayer. Society may dismiss it, but God doesn't. In fact, He places a premium on it, so take advantage of that gift He gives all of us and lift your parents up in prayer on a regular basis.

Keep in mind that honoring your parents is more about you than about them. Honor is not about whether others deserve it; honor is about you. Are you someone who treats people honorably or not? When you are one who honors others because you choose to do what's right, rather than constantly judging whether or not someone deserves it, showing honor becomes much easier.

DAY 2
Be Happy

Author and radio host Dennis Prager says, "Happiness is a moral obligation."[13] By that, he's referring to what we'd call "joy," not "pleasure." He goes on to state that "happy people make the world better, and unhappy people make it worse." If you think about it, it's hard to argue with that last part. If you've been around unhappy people, you know what a beating it is. On the other hand, happy people are so much easier to work with, be around, and generally tolerate. (Unless you're unhappy, then they can be extremely annoying!)

Clearly, it's best to genuinely be happy and show it. But what about when we're not that happy? Is it okay to let everyone around us know how unhappy we are? I would agree with Prager and say, "No." Especially at home.

I admit, I haven't always done this. Early in my marriage, I would bring my work-related frustrations and dissatisfactions home and dump them on my wife. She graciously listened most days. On days she might argue or push back, it just inflated my unhappiness, not to mention hers when I reacted negatively. One day, I heard Dennis Prager make his point about happiness being a "moral obligation," and it was like a slap in the face. *What the heck have I been doing?* I thought. My need to vent was an ugly, self-centered expression that gave zero consideration to my wife. I realized that regardless of how my day went at the office, she deserved a happy husband walking through the door, even if I didn't feel like it. So I tried it. What a difference it made! I found that even when I was completely faking it, her response to my outward attitude began to change my feelings. It is within our power to shift moods. It turned out that acting happy led to more happiness for both of us. Just looking cheerful brought joy to my heart.

Some people don't like the word *happiness*. Christians often set it up as the opposite of holiness. But what could bring more joy than a right relationship with our Creator? Use the word *joy* if it's clearer or more compatible with your connotation of the word. The point is that a glad heart shows on your face and lifts up those around you. Children need a happy parent. Husbands and wives need a joyful spouse. Our happiness affects everyone around us.

I'm not suggesting that bad things should make us happy. I'm saying that we should learn to handle them in a way that doesn't cause collateral damage to those around us. If you need to vent, establish the appropriate time and place beforehand. Maybe you have a friend you can text and request a phone call with the express purpose of venting on your way home from work so that the day's frustrations are off your chest when you get home. If your spouse is agreeable, simply set the conversation up. "Honey, I need to vent; is this a good time for you?" It's amazing how this simple preface changes the response (unless you are venting about your spouse).

In addition to the words you communicate, listen to your tone. Most of us are tone deaf to ourselves. We sound one way to ourselves and another to the rest of the world. If you are experiencing this disconnect, just record yourself in normal conversation. If the fact that you are recording doesn't make you aware of how you sound, play it back. You might be shocked. I'm convinced that the tone we use, along with the body language expressed while talking, actually communicates more than the words we choose. It's nearly impossible to communicate in a book, but try saying the phrase "you look great" or "everything is fine" in as many different ways possible, and you will get an idea.

We all know people that elevate the mood when they walk in a room, and we all know people that bring it down. I don't think that unhappy people realize the damage they do to their loved ones. Discontent, bitterness, anger, and every other enemy of happiness make life much more difficult. It crushes the spirits of others. If you're a miserable person, don't look for company. Get help!

I fully believe that it is not only proper, but essential to act and speak in a way that contributes to the happiness of others *even when we are not happy ourselves*. Perhaps more so in that case. Yes, we should seek to resolve the issues bringing us down, but until then we have no business bringing everyone else down.

Happiness in you will create an environment for happiness in other people. Your family needs that. You owe it to them to find inner joy. It's a light that brightens everyone's day. Be that light.

DAY 3
Be Patient

Nothing tests your patience like living in close quarters. The global 2020 quarantine proved that. The internet memes were great, but the rise in cases of domestic abuse was heartbreaking. For many, it truly tested their patience.

Here's one of the most underrated truths when it comes to having an enjoyable, stable family: It's better to master patience than it is to advance in your career, make a ton of money, achieve fame, or any other measure of success we normally identify. Why? Because losing control destroys relationships. Even if it's not full-blown temper tantrums, the steady irritation amounts to death by a thousand cuts. Impatience either explodes in a catastrophic mess or chips away until your family cracks and crumbles.

Patience takes practice. We can easily take our household for granted. It doesn't come naturally for most people, so self-awareness is required. If you don't know where you stand with your family, consider asking them. Take the response or responses quietly. Don't defend yourself—that will likely shut them down. If you find that they perceive you as impatient, employ these tactics to begin developing patience within yourself.

First, give others the benefit of the doubt. Don't assume that a comment is intended as an insult. If necessary, ask point-blank, "Is that intended as an insult?" If it was not, that will allow the other person to explain. If it was intentional, you have effectively called out their unacceptable behavior. That won't take the sting out of it, but it will at least provide some clarity as to who is escalating the tension. If that is a pattern, then you will need to bring in a third party to help resolve some issues. Reacting by losing your cool just makes it worse.

Second, don't take slowness or inaction as defiance. If a child routinely fails in an area, like doing homework or chores, deal with it before you lose your patience. Take the time to figure out the problem while you are thinking clearly. If they are lacking in an area and need to change, help them instead of badgering or belittling them. Try to see things from their perspective. Avoid the self-centered view that everything they do that isn't up to your standards is somehow directed at you. Even when you're certain that it is, address the situation with calm and composure. Extending kindness and grace to others lays the foundation for an atmosphere of patience. If discipline is needed, do it without anger. That means confronting it well before your patience runs out.

Third, think before you speak. Ask yourself, *Will the words that come out of my mouth make things better or worse?* There is great power in your words. Sharp words create or increase tension and strife. A kind word provides relief. Master your emotions, and you will master your words.

Fourth, don't return impatience with more impatience. Recognize it in others, and know that it is wrong. This is key in dealing with it, both in others and in yourself. When you perceive impatience on the part of someone else and identify it as such, you can control your own response to it. Choose to respond in the right way, not in an equally wrong way. Try smiling and holding your tongue. It may irritate the other person, but it will keep you from being sucked deeper into a pit of negativity.

Finally, pay attention to your body language. Impatience can be communicated as strongly by non-verbal cues as your words. Controlling your mouth is a good start, but if your shoulders tense, eyes roll, and lungs exhale loudly, that communicates impatience. Master everything—mind, body, and spirit. This is one case where it's all right to "fake it until you make it," as long as you're aware that you're battling it. It's all right to protect your family from your personal struggles when you're actively working through it. When you can't do that on your own, ask for God's help.

There is power in patience. It is primarily the power of yourself. Making self-control a discipline will serve you well in every area because it is power over your circumstances. When situations drive you to impatience, you lose control over them. Learning the art of patience allows you to better face every situation, thinking more clearly and acting in ways that don't result in damaging consequences. Patience is more than a virtue; it is a powerful weapon against the things that would seek to destroy you and your family.

DAY 4
Make Peace at Home

Tornadoes are a perennial threat where I live. A few years ago, 10 different ones touched down in one day, causing more damage than any storm in recent memory and costing more than any in state history. People were displaced, lives were disrupted for weeks, and the cleanup consumed an incredible amount of time and energy.

A home without peace is even worse. It causes all sorts of damage. It can displace family members, disrupt lives for years, and require a huge amount of time and energy to repair. The havoc created by a tumultuous household can ripple through generations. That's why peace is paramount for everyone living together under one roof. If you're single, you only need to live at peace with yourself (which can be a challenge unto itself), but if you are part of a family, the dynamics expand to every member of your household.

A peaceful home is a refuge in a stormy world. The stresses that come from outside the home, whether at work or school, can only be properly handled when the home offers shelter from them. We all need a place to rest. If it's not inside the home, we either live in a constant state of tension or we look elsewhere, which usually drives a family apart. We also need a place where we can learn what peace looks like, otherwise we can start to believe that disorder is normal. When we have a peaceful home, we have a compass to navigate through the pressures of the world and an anchor to keep us from being driven by every wind.

Peace doesn't come without effort. It must be made. An awareness and a conscious effort to cultivate it are required for peace to become a reality. When you work to make peace, you will see good things happen.

Here are some practical steps that will help create a more peaceful home:

Respond, don't react.

Conflict will arise. Don't be surprised by this. When it happens, take a moment to consider your reply. What you do next will determine the direction the conversation moves. Take control of the situation as best you can and look for a resolution. You can't be responsible for how others handle conflict, but you can learn to control how you handle it. Know that you are doing the right thing by working to settle it.

Confront when necessary.

Peace is always the goal but not at the expense of legitimate problems. Paradoxically, confrontation is necessary to achieve peace. Burying real problems creates a false peace, which is never healthy. The United States did this with the issue of slavery from its foundation until the Civil War. Compromises were made in the writing of the Constitution in 1787. It did allow for the abolition of the slave trade 21 years after its inception, so on January 1, 1808, President Thomas Jefferson's bill prohibiting "the importation of slaves into any port or place within the jurisdiction of the United States," also approved by Congress, became law. It ended the transatlantic trade, but it did nothing to end slavery. As the nation expanded westward, adding new states, the dithering continued. The Missouri Compromise of 1820, the Compromise of 1850 (dealing with California, Utah, and New Mexico), and the Kansas-Nebraska Act of 1854 all delayed the inevitable confrontation that would only be resolved by the Civil War. An estimated 620,000 men died in battle. Hundreds of thousands more died of disease. Cities burned, and crops were destroyed. Refusing to confront the evil of slavery sooner cost the lives and wealth of whites, both those who supported slavery as well as the prohibitionists who opposed it. History does not accurately record the damage done to generations of slaves who suffered cruelly and unjustly, but it is obvious that they paid the highest price of anyone.

Even after President Abraham Lincoln signed the Emancipation Proclamation in 1862, the systemic oppression continued for another century. Voter suppression continued despite two amendments to the Constitution and multiple civil rights acts. Public segregation was not outlawed until 1964. The Civil Rights Act of 1968 capped off a decade of drastic improvements, ending legalized discrimination, and enforcement legislation continued to move forward for decades. Even so, we are still wrestling with serious issues today—all because confrontation gets put off until tension boils over. Don't do this in your home. Deal with legitimate issues before a war breaks out.

Put a little grace in your words.

Being "right" is not always sufficient. Preserving a relationship should be the priority, even while refusing to compromise principles. This tension demands grace. Take the time to listen to others and articulate your position. A little understanding goes a long way. You may not reach agreement, but you can at least have clarity.

Certain situations will be impossible to resolve. A child selling narcotics out of the house, a husband physically abusing a wife, and other incompatible scenarios demand hard lines and, usually, separation. But most conflicts are on a much lesser scale. When you let someone know that you disagree with something, let them know twice as much that you still love them. This allows at least a thread of relationship to hold while offering them a lifeline back if their decisions cause them pain. Truth and grace must go hand-in-hand. Allow truth to maintain the integrity of your home while allowing grace to cover the mistakes.

Go out of your way to do something nice for others.

Setting aside time to demonstrate kindness speaks volumes, even in the little things—perhaps especially in the little things. Do it without expecting anything in return. Do it even when they may not notice or acknowledge it. Selfless giving has its own rewards and lays a foundation for peaceful coexistence.

Finally, make others smile.

Well-timed levity is good. It can knock the edge off of tension and brighten someone's mood. Self-deprecating humor, where you poke fun at yourself, can shift a person's attitude in a better direction when used properly. Laughter can open an avenue to meaningful, serious conversation. It is an art, but when employed effectively, it can help resolve real issues.

Whenever it is within your power, seek peace with everyone, especially at home. The world is tumultuous enough on its own. Our homes desperately need to be a refuge of peace.

DAY 5
Don't Worry

There are tons of pithy and insightful quotes telling us we should not worry about things. But given the world we live in and the people we love, isn't there ample reason to worry? Any parent can tell you that children provide frequent opportunities to worry. Sickness, accident, crime, rebellion, self-harm . . . the list is long. If you genuinely care about others, especially your family, there is cause for concern. And therein lies the difference: concern vs. worry.

Worry is anxiety created by something that has not happened. It causes more problems than it solves precisely because it doesn't solve anything. Medical experts tell us that it can even cause problems with digestion, sleep, breathing, and heart health.[14] Worry over something not real can become very real and very damaging.

Concern, on the other hand, motivates us to solve a potential problem. Worry frets about a car accident that has not occurred. Concern checks the tires, brakes, and other critical parts. Worry harps on the teenage driver. Concern instructs and prepares.

My daughter's rental house in her college town was broken into in broad daylight. None of the four girls who live there were at home, but the thieves went through their closets and drawers, taking random things of value. Worse than the loss of property and cash was the loss of security. For several days, their anxiety impacted everything they did. They wouldn't stay at home alone. They looked over their shoulders walking to their cars when leaving for class. Every noise at night sounded like a threat. The thieves were caught and some of their items were returned, but the violation left them feeling vulnerable again.

As parents, my wife and I are always concerned for our children's safety. They are covered by roadside assistance in case they break down. (All of their vehicles have over 100,000 miles, so that is a legitimate concern!) We bought the girls pepper spray. We instructed them on basic safety. We pray. A lot. But this break-in demanded more than concern. Worry would not help. Only action would. So we booked a hotel room on a Saturday night in the college town, drove down for the weekend, and installed wireless cameras all around the house. At the touch of an app, we could see all of the entrances, the parking area, and the sides of the house. We gave my daughter and all of her roommates access to the app, so they could see, hear, and talk to anyone outside of their house from anywhere. Granted, it wouldn't stop someone who was determined to break in, but they would be on camera, which is a strong deterrent for petty thieves.

Our concern will never go away—and it shouldn't—but we don't stay up nights worrying about any of our children. We have taken steps to address potential issues, and we rest in that knowledge. Imagining all of the terrible things that could happen, and have happened to others, is a weight none of us can bear.

Alex Honnold was the first (and only, to date) person to "free solo" El Capitan in Yosemite National Park. That means climbing a vertical cliff over 3,000 feet high with no ropes. Just "shoes and a chalk bag." It's 2 1/2 times as tall as the Empire State Building and if you fall, you die. In a 2018 TED Talk, Honnold talked about the mental aspect of climbing without a rope. "Staying calm and performing at your best, when you know that any mistake could mean death, requires a certain kind of mindset."[15] That line elicited laughter from the crowd. Most of us would call that mindset "insane." But for Honnold, his years of experience and practice on the wall gave him the knowledge and confidence to make it happen. Because he had trained, studied, and fully prepared, he had no anxiety. As he defied death in a feat performed by no other human being, he wasn't worried.

We all defy death every day, though not in as dramatic fashion. We drive on roads where others have perished. We eat daily meals, even though people occasionally get food poisoning. We walk among strangers, even though in my country nearly one-third of the adult working age population has a criminal record.[16] Danger may be all around, but we take normal precautions to minimize it. We can also refuse to be suffocated by worrying about things completely out of our control that may or may not happen. If something is a concern, take action and take comfort.

The Apostle Paul urges followers of Christ, "Be anxious for nothing, but in everything by prayer and supplication with thanksgiving let your requests be made known to God. And the peace of God, which surpasses all comprehension, will guard your hearts and your minds in Christ Jesus" (Philippians 4:6-7 NASB). Peter tells us to cast our anxiety on Jesus (see 1 Peter 5:7), which means to place it on Him the way you might set a hot plate on a potholder. Worry will burn you, but Jesus can buffer us from the pain if we will let Him. He himself said, "So do not worry about tomorrow; for tomorrow will care for itself" (Matthew 6:34 NASB).

Worry really is a choice we make. We can take care of legitimate concerns and leave the rest to God. Or we can let our imaginations run wild, replaying scenes of worst-case scenarios until we weigh down ourselves and everyone around us. Worry is a burden we were not built to carry and never designed to put on others. Especially our family.

DAY 6
Drink from Your Own Well

In ancient cultures with desert climates, they had a saying: "Drink water from your own well." Water was more precious than anything else. It gave life to crops, animals, and people. Digging a well required long, hard work with no guarantee of success. A family with a quality well had something of great value. One of the worst offenses you could commit would be to steal someone else's water.

The most destructive force in today's families is the urge to "drink from someone else's well." That is, to engage in sexual activity outside of marriage. This notion is often viewed as constricting, prudish, or outdated. But the truth of the matter is that the one who commits adultery is an utter fool, for it destroys the person engaging in it while causing severe damage to everyone close. Marriages struggle to recover or, most often, fall apart. Children are forced to endure their parents' messy emotions and straddle multiple families. Reputations are tarnished. Deep wounds are inflicted.

The road back to trust and stability can be long and difficult. Many don't make it. People can do their best to cope and walk through it, but there's no doubt that it causes pain. Avoiding that path altogether is by far the superior way.

The Apostle Paul told the church in Thessalonica that "this is the will of God, your sanctification; that is, that you abstain from sexual immorality" (see 1 Thessalonians 4:3 NASB). The Greek word there is *porneia*, a broad term including adultery, fornication, homosexuality, prostitution, bestiality, incest, and every other illicit sexual action. If you believe that Paul was just close-minded because of his cultural background or that God is some sort of cosmic killjoy, you might not take that seriously. But if you honestly look at how those things impact people, you must admit that they work to undermine the family unit. And if you believe that God is love—not just a loving God, but the very essence of love itself—then you will begin to see that these boundaries begin to work in your favor. It is for your own good, as well as for the benefit of those around you. Abstaining from sexual immorality is abstaining from poison. Yes, you have the freedom to drink it, but you are not immune to the consequences.

Wholeness only comes when we are not fractured or broken by the things that destroy relationships. God wants wholeness for us; therefore, it is His will that we abstain from all forms of sexual immorality. At the same time, this idea of not drinking from someone else's well implies that you *should* drink from your own. Sex is not something to be avoided or vilified. God came up with the idea. He gave it to married couples for enjoyment. Without it, there is no such thing as children, so it obviously is a significant factor in creating families. It should be enjoyed and celebrated in its proper context, which is within the covenant relationship of one man and one woman. Construct your own well and drink liberally!

Another aspect of a good well is that it is built properly. That requires two things: work and design. Marriage requires work. A fatal mistake of many men is thinking that once a woman is courted and captured, the challenge is conquered. That's part of the reason some look for another conquest outside of marriage. But women were never meant to be captured or conquered. Marriage is designed to be a lifelong journey. The commitment to walk that road together requires effort. The walk down the aisle is merely the beginning of that journey, not the end. Some parts of the adventure are difficult. The road can be rough, and bandits will try to steal what you have. Vigilance and determination are required. There will be times when you have to fight to stay on your path. But it's better than walking alone, and it can lead to wonderful places.

Design means intentionality. The more purpose put into it, the stronger and longer lasting it will be. If you use well-crafted stones or bricks in a proven pattern, your well can go deeper, where the best water is, and hold up through the storms and dry seasons. Building a strong marriage, with depth and stability, only comes by deliberately following a pattern of love, respect, self-sacrifice, patience, and support. Shallow wells sour or dry up. Deep ones provide refreshment and sustenance for a lifetime.

By the way, you'll likely notice other people's wells. Maybe the stones or bricks are newer and prettier. The bucket might be bigger. But more impressive does not mean better. The well you construct will always be best for you. Don't start staring at other wells and comparing them to yours. They may *seem* better, but for all you know, the water is poison. You know that the water in your well is pure, so it's guaranteed to taste better and keep you healthy. Stick with it, enjoy it, and be content.

DAY 7
Make Them Cry at Your Funeral

There are two things I want at my funeral: few friends and distraught loved ones. I don't want my friends to be there because I want to outlive them all. And I want my children, grandchildren, and other loved ones to cry their eyes out because they will miss me so much.

This may sound a bit morbid, but the reality is that we have happy memories of good people, while those who are not so good fade from mind. In some sad situations, it's a relief when someone passes. Trust me—you don't want to be that person.

Obituaries can be odd things. They state the facts: birth location, education, occupation, and date of death. They recount relationships: parents, spouse, and children. They usually mention a few things the person enjoyed or spent time doing, like hobbies or volunteering. It's a brief distillation of our lives.

What will yours say? "He spent long hours at the office." "She gave them a piece of her mind." "He loved golf more than his wife." "She protected herself by shutting people out." "He cheated several times." "She drank away her problems." God forbid!

There are two common problems for families trying to write an obit. On one end of the spectrum, a few words don't do the person justice. Statements that seem trite like, like "she loved her family" or "he liked to help others," fail to convey the depth of the truth. On the other end, nice words can be hard to come up with. I want the first problem for my family, not the second.

I want my life to be so full that a couple of paragraphs can't contain them. I want them to say something like, "he raised his children right." But more than that, I want everyone who knows my children to see it. I want my efforts at home to outlive me by generations. I want my work writing books, working for a ministry, and contributing to mission outreaches to continue having an effect far beyond the grave. I want my volunteer time at church to contribute to a stronger body of Christ, even though largely unnoticed by most people. The dash between my birth year and death year needs to be fat with eternal impact.

Most people die and disappear, but the life lived well has visible ripples far into the future. The good news is that it's never too late to turn things around. You can start leaving a legacy today by making every moment count, touching others with words and acts built on love, kindness, and truth. You can motivate people to do and be better than they realize. It's amazing how many people change the world after having their world changed by just one person.

Everybody knows of Dr. Martin Luther King, Jr., but most have never heard of Rev. Vernon Johns. He preceded Dr. King at Dexter Avenue Baptist Church, teaching King how to stand up to racial injustice. In the words of Dr. King, Rev. Johns "never allowed an injustice to come to his attention without speaking out against it."[17] If it weren't for that one man, the other man would not have had the global and historical impact that he had.

The series of movies comprising *The Lord of the Rings* and *The Chronicles of Narnia* have been seen by millions, but few know the man who inspired both J.R.R. Tolkien and C.S. Lewis. His name was George MacDonald, a Scottish minister, author, and poet. He wrote numerous allegories, though few know them today. Yet if it weren't for his efforts, we may not know the works of those two famous men who have inspired millions.

One person can make a difference, whether in the life of one or the lives of millions. So, make them cry at your funeral, and inspire them for the rest of their lives.

WEEK 6

"A man of words and not of deeds,
is like a garden full of weeds."

—BENJAMIN FRANKLIN

UPGRADE
Your Works

Once you get your thoughts right, your actions will follow. Trying to do good things before setting your mind in the proper direction never works. Sure, you might do something nice once in a while, but it only comes naturally when your heart and mind don't have to fight themselves to act in a certain way. Healthy bees naturally produce honey. Watered vines automatically produce tasty grapes. And good thoughts instinctively lead to better works.

What exactly do "better works" look like? Ask a dozen different people what counts as a good work and you'll likely get a dozen different answers. Buying coffee for the person behind you. Rescuing an animal from a shelter. Giving money to charity. Reposting something online to raise awareness.

Maybe it's something "big." Stopping an assault. Building a home for a handicapped person. Adopting a child. Saving a drowning child. Providing a needed relationship.

All of these things are good, no doubt. But how can we perform "better works" on a daily basis in subtle and meaningful ways? It's not as hard as you might think, but once your thinking is in order, these seven characteristics will define your life.

DAY 1
Be Good

I have an affinity for mayonnaise with olive oil. Think about it: a regular turkey and cheese sandwich goes to the next level with a little olive oil mayonnaise. Seriously. It goes from being average to being really good. And the thing is, you don't really notice the mayo unless it's not there. You don't take a bite and think, *Wow, what great mayonnaise!* No, you take a bite and think, *That's a good turkey and cheese sandwich!* The mayo is there in the background, making everything better without stealing the glory from the main ingredients. Why? Because it's good.

Goodness in a person is a little like olive oil mayonnaise. It makes life better without demanding attention. Astute people will notice it and may even point it out. The purpose of goodness is not to be praised by others. Doing good is simply helping someone.

Making it a part of everyday life takes *doing* good one step further to *being* good. This requires awareness of those around you, caring about their needs as much or more than your own. Caring means demonstrating it. When you see an opportunity, take it. Don't withhold it when it's in your power to help. It can be as simple as holding a door open for a stranger, assisting at work when it's not required, offering a ride to someone, or sharing a meal.

True goodness exists for the benefit of others. It is not a show of virtue. Doing good things in order to impress others undermines the very meaning of goodness. Many authentic acts of goodness go unnoticed by everyone except those on the receiving end. That's okay. A light in the darkness shines on its own. Whether one person or a million see it doesn't matter. The point is not the adulation you receive from others because of your goodness. The point is that goodness shapes you into a better person. If you have to brag about your goodness, then it has spoiled. Your mayonnaise is way beyond the expiration date and what should be a good thing now tastes bad. But true goodness makes everything "next level."

Common decency is not so common these days. That's because people are a conflicted mess of self-serving attitudes, identity confusion, and internal turmoil. Even so, a surprising percentage of people respond to basic goodness. It's like a flame that lights a bigger fire. If you're good to someone else, they are more inclined to be good as well. Of course, some won't be, but that's their problem not yours. Lighting that fire of goodness by displaying common decency inspires more warmth and light. It also wins people over to your side. True good deeds are like seeds growing into a garden of friendships.

To instill goodness into your life, start within. If you start with exterior measures of goodness, you'll fall into one of several traps. If your goodness goes unnoticed, you'll likely feel resentment. *Don't others see how much I'm doing for them? Why don't people appreciate everything I do?* And just like that, your attempt at goodness turns into bitterness.

Or you might receive the full attention you think you deserve. Admirers might throw a banquet to give you an award, shout your praises all over Twitter, and make you a reality show star. You'll think, *I earned this fame because I do better things than other people!* And just like that, you're deep in the pit of pride and self-righteousness—and you probably won't know it.

Or you might realize that most people are not as good as you. Then you might begin letting them know it. *Why can't you be more like me? You're going straight to hell!* And just like that, nobody wants to be around you. You have set your own trap of judgmentalism and walked right into it.

Much of goodness is simply being nice. Being nice expresses itself in attitude, words, and deeds. When you treat others the way you want to be treated, even when they don't return the favor, you position yourself to receive better treatment from others. Cruelty destroys people, but kindness is its own reward. When you are nice to people, you avoid arguments, animosity, and anger. A kind word sweetens people's moods, relieves the pressure they might be feeling, and encourages goodness in them. At worst, you have the peace of knowing that you were decent and kind, even when others don't respond. At best, you influence others to be kind, cultivating an atmosphere of goodness.

Goodness is a bit of an odd thing. It doesn't manifest as much when you focus on it but instead when you focus on others. You're pursuing it and you're aware of it, but you're concerned less about your own goodness and more on what you can do for others. The motive is pure, which only comes from a place of purity. To achieve goodness, you must first pursue purity of heart. Then the good things you do are not just *doing* good, but *being* good. The honor you seek is that which you can show to others, not what you can obtain for yourself. This starts by simply asking yourself what you can do to help that person next to you, then doing it, and looking for the next opportunity.

Open your eyes to the opportunities around you. They are there, waiting for you to take advantage of them. Do some good and before too long, you will be good.

DAY 2
Be Honest

In 1929, Simon & Schuster published *The Cradle of the Deep*, a riveting childhood memoir by Joan Lowell. She told of being spirited away by her sea captain father as an infant to grow up on the sea. Her tale took readers across the Pacific and South Seas aboard the trading ship *Minnie A. Caine*, where she was tutored by an old sailmaker named Stitches, fraternized with salty, fighting men, learned native dialects in exotic places, harpooned a whale, and witnessed a shark eating a man alive. It ended when the *Minnie* wrecked off the coast of Australia and Joan, now 17 years old, had to swim to shore with her three pet kittens clinging to her back.

It became an immediate bestseller. The *Los Angeles Times* raved about it. The *Saturday Evening Post* published an essay about her lessons at sea. It was featured in the national Book-of-the-Month Club. It sold over 100,000 copies, and movie legend D.W. Griffith signed her to star in a film based on her exploits. The success of the memoir more than justified the $50,000 (almost three-quarters of a million in today's dollars) she received from the publisher.

Unfortunately, it was all a lie. Joan Lowell grew up in Berkeley. Her father was a sea captain, but she had only been on a few short rides on his boat. The *Minnie A. Caine* was still intact in an Oakland dock.[18,19] It was such a national scandal that even Will

Rogers made jokes about her.

Sometimes, it seems like it's easier to lie. Those lies can become a framework in which we live, but there are only two outcomes to such an existence: prison or collapse. Most people don't begin with a big lie, like Lowell, but with small ones. We lie to ourselves or to others in slight, often meaningless ways. But like a paper brick stacked on another paper brick, a habit of lying constructs a false world. That's why it's important to adopt a personal policy of truth down to the minute detail.

Honesty is more than the alternative to lying; it is a reliable guide for good people. Honesty will direct your life in such a way that you never have to worry about being locked in a cell of falsehoods or crushed when your world crumbles. You can walk through each day securely, never fearing that you will be discovered and exposed, because truth stands firm.

Unfortunately, our culture has perverted honesty. The phrase, "I'm not gonna lie . . . " is often followed by something harsh, unflattering, or cruel. Being unkind in the name of honesty is not virtuous; it just reveals the ugliness inside the speaker's heart. Sure, honesty can be tough, but it's not a weapon to be wielded in a fit of self-righteousness.

I see most of the comments on our television program's You-Tube channel. There are some mean people out there! One person commented on a show clip featuring a female author, "I have to be honest. Her hair looks awful. She shouldn't be seen in public." That's not honesty; that's just ugly. Tact is not a required sacrifice on the altar of honesty.

Real honesty lays the foundation for healthy relationships. It provides an atmosphere for clarity and conversation. Even when honesty is difficult, it's a better alternative to hiding the truth. A hard truth that isn't spoken allows people to be blissfully unaware of something important or it forces them to speculate about what you're not telling them. Both of those scenarios create more of a mess than putting a tough truth on the table—as tactfully as possible, of course.

Trust is an absolute requirement in lasting relationships. Lies are the fast lane to destroying trust. Scottish novelist Walter Scott wrote, "What a tangled web we weave when first we practice to deceive." Once deceit is discovered—and it always is—the road back to trust is long and difficult. Some relationships are never untangled. But honesty protects valued relationships.

Perhaps the most common lie is the one told to avoid confrontation. Maybe you've had a version of this conversation:

"Are you all right?"

"Yes."

"Are you sure? Something seems to be bothering you."

"No, everything is fine."

It's easy to justify that one, but think about what you're doing when you take the easy out. Ducking it with a lie can send multiple messages, none of which may be true. It can say, "Our relationship isn't important enough to have a hard conversation." It could communicate, "I don't trust you enough to be honest with you." Or it might convey, "You're not worth my time."

Confrontation is necessary in relationships, but it must be done with kindness, gentleness, and love. An honest answer—even if it's something like, "I'm not able to have this conversation right now, but we will later"—at least avoids the damage of the "I'm fine" dodge.

Honesty requires two things: integrity and sincerity. Both can and must occur simultaneously. Integrity provides the necessary message to communicate, while sincerity brings the best way to communicate it. Usually the message is spoken in words, but body language and tone play an important part. Consider the words, "It really offends me when you say things like that." When spoken softly, but firmly, it can be a powerful wakeup call for the person hearing it. When screamed with clenched fists, it feels more like an unhinged accusation.

Actions also convey meaning. The words "I'm sorry" mean nothing when your actions contradict them. Conversely, changing your offensive ways speaks volumes.

Honesty is less about your words and more about your lifestyle. When you live honestly, your mouth will follow suit. That requires purity of heart and mind, which is where the real battle rages. Purge your heart and mind of deception, secrecy, and manipulation, and honesty will come naturally.

DAY 3
Be Generous

Christmas is the season we normally associate with generosity. We shop, we wrap, we bake, we give. It's a wonderful time to be generous with those we love and even a few strangers. Charities have also figured out that early December is the best time for a big push, which has adopted the name "Giving Tuesday." It has grown to an estimated $2 billion in total donations for various non-profit organizations.[20] Despite the cultural divisions, we are still generous.

This is a good thing. Generosity is more than an admirable virtue; it is a characteristic of the highest order. While the act of gift-giving is an obvious expression, there are many more ways to give generously throughout the year, including some that don't involve cash.

"Time is money," Benjamin Franklin once wrote. The sentiment predates him by centuries, but the idea that our time has value means that we can be generous with our time in ways that rival finances. It's easy to take people for granted, but understanding that time is short should help us view it as a commodity to be spent wisely. Investing encouragement, comfort, joy, and love in family and close friends places the proper value of these moments. Spending quality time with loved ones is priceless.

Giving yourself in service to others, whether by volunteering, taking meals to someone in need, helping at work when it's not your responsibility, or a myriad of other ways, is also a gift. Actions speak loudly. The fact that you would spend hours doing something that benefits others when you could be taking that time for yourself tells them that they are important and valuable. People may not remember the words you speak, but they will remember the things you do. The selflessness of purely tending to another's needs with no tangible reward for yourself leaves an indelible mark on someone's soul.

Another facet of generosity is giving your talent. Each of us has inherent gifts and abilities. We use these to provide for ourselves and family, but we can also use them to help others. This, too, is an act of generosity. If you're an accountant, help a single mother with her taxes. If you're a teacher, tutor a refugee who is adapting to a new culture. If you bake cookies, take some to a homeless shelter. If you're a dancer, perform at a nursing home. Be creative. You have something that can aid, inspire, educate, or entertain. You have something that someone else needs. Be generous with your talent.

Giving a gift can open doors. There are many ways that an act of generosity can create an opportunity for relationship. I've seen someone give a waiter a shockingly large tip, then watched that waiter open up about his financial difficulties and family struggles, which allowed a time of comfort and counsel that doesn't normally happen in restaurants. I've witnessed a teenager volunteer to take care of the lawn of a couple who had spent several weeks going back and forth from the hospital with a family member who was suffering. That led to more opportunities for other neighbors to step in and help during their time of need. The community grew closer and stronger. A few years ago, a Jewish cemetery in Philadelphia was vandalized. People from various backgrounds and faiths converged on the scene to help clean up and stand up against the hateful act.[21] In the middle of the COVID-19 pandemic, numerous photos and videos circulated social media to document creative ways people helped others cope with the lockdown. Countless stories exist where a simple unexpected gift created an opportunity for a valuable encounter. When you develop a sense of awareness, you will find ample opportunities to utilize an act of generosity to create new relationships and strengthen existing ones.

Paul instructed the early church "to do good, to be rich in good works, to be generous and ready to share . . . " (1 Timothy 6:18 NASB). Generosity was designed to be less about charity and more about church. For Christians, it should be routine, not rare. People claiming the name of Christ must be known as givers, not takers. The world needs to know, experience, and feel the impact of God's followers. This can happen when we generously give our time, talent, and treasure.

Generosity does not "give to get." However, there are definite benefits for the giver because it unlocks the blessings of heaven. "The generous will prosper; those who refresh others will themselves be refreshed" (Proverbs 11:25 NLT). "Good will come to those who are generous and lend freely . . ." (Psalm 112:5). Many verses affirm this truth. Jesus emphasized it on several occasions. When we are generous, God sees it and rewards it. *How* He rewards it is entirely up to Him. His rewards transcend the temporary physical things, though we may receive those too. Rest in the assurance that He is good and wise, giving us what we need beyond what we can imagine.

I think God places a premium on generosity because giving reflects His very character. "For God so loved the world, he *gave* . . . " (see John 3:16). There is no better model than that! Emulating Him invites the richness of the Holy Spirit, who pours out Himself on us to satisfy our souls. Establishing a lifetime habit of generosity blesses others, provides refreshment for yourself, and glorifies

God in your good works. Let people say what they will of you, but make sure they can say that you are generous.

DAY 4
Help the Poor

There is a difference between giving and lending. Giving to the poor is an act of charity. You give to help someone, expecting no return. A "thank you" is nice. Maybe there are tears. They might even make a reality show with a big reveal. But usually, you give and only get the satisfaction of doing a good thing.

Lending, on the other hand, puts someone in debt to you. They agree to accept your money and pay you back with interest. You give up something of value for a period of time, knowing you will get something in return. That "something" will be better than what you sacrificed for the term of the loan.

Proverbs says, "If you help the poor, you are lending to the Lord—and he will repay you!" (19:17 NLT). That means God owes you. Now don't get me wrong, God doesn't inherently owe any human anything. Instead, He established a contract and agreed to the terms of the loan. You help the poor, and He agrees to repay you.

When we break down the original language in that verse, we see it is not specifically about money. The action to *help* can be translated "to show grace" or "to show favor." The *poor* person is one who is "weak, needy, or low."

Helping someone in need or in a low place may mean giving money to a charity that feeds the hungry or provides shelter to the homeless, but it could also be expressed in many other ways. Believe me, a rich person can be in a low place. Showing grace to that person devastated by divorce, loss, addiction, or any other condition that crushes the human soul is an act of helping the "poor."

When we do such things, we "lend" to God. That word also means "to join with." It's common for people to ask God to join them in their endeavors and that's good, but a fast way to be on God's side is to help someone in need. He has already said that He is there, so we can jump right into God's will by joining with Him in the work He is doing in the lives of people. When we do, He "repays" us— not necessarily in monetary terms (that's fairly low on His list of good gifts), but by rewarding us however He wishes. And trust me, when God rewards you, it is better than anything you can imagine.

Related ideas contained in that word *repay* are "to make whole" and "to be in a covenant of peace." When you show favor to someone who is weak, needy, or low, you enter into a covenant of peace with God. He agrees to make you whole. That's huge. In a society that pays millions of dollars a year to psychiatrists and counselors, peace and wholeness can be found when we join with God to help those who are suffering. That is something money can't buy!

The flip side is not good. "Those who shut their ears to the cries of the poor will be ignored in their own time of need" (Proverbs 21:13 NLT). The same Hebrew word for *poor* is used in both verses. The choice is clear: help those in need and be joined with God; or ignore them and be ignored in your time of need. Do you ever feel like your needs are not being met? Then look to help someone else and let God do His part. He has already promised that He would.

Deciding whether or not to help those in need also presents another choice. "Those who oppress the poor insult their Maker, but helping the poor honors him" (Proverbs 14:31 NLT). When you put it that way, it makes it easy to reach out to the oppressed. (By the way, *poor* is once again translated from the same word used in the previous scriptures.) No matter what mistakes you have made in life, it is never too late to begin honoring God by helping someone in need. He notices. He sees it and takes action. He redeems the lost time to make good things happen in your life. That is His character that He anxiously waits to express through you.

You can't go wrong by helping people who are having a difficult time in life. Show a little favor to that one who has no friends. Buy lunch for that co-worker whose spouse just left. Give someone a ride to the doctor or hospital. People are hurting, and you can comfort them. These simple acts put you in God's will. Cash in on the promise that He is on your side, and honor Him.

DAY 5
Be Fair

Fairness is a term thrown around loosely these days. Society abuses it, twisting it into a tool for bizarre favoritism. In the name of fairness, boys who "identify as girls" compete for athletic scholarships with actual girls, which is anything but fair.

Merriam-Webster defines *fair* as "marked by impartiality and honesty: free from self-interest, prejudice, or favoritism." It is important to distinguish between equality and fairness. Equality is completely blind to the individual, treating everyone exactly the same way. In an equal race, a 10-year-old competes directly with a 25-year-old. In a strictly equal work environment, the janitor makes the same salary as the CEO. There is harsh legalism inherent in an overly zealous atmosphere of equality.

Such zeal led to the life sentence of a woman named Alice Marie Johnson. She was presented with an "opportunity" at a time in her life when she was devastated by divorce and living under extreme financial pressure. An acquaintance asked her to receive phone calls at her Memphis home, which would give her coded information that she would pass on to another phone call. She was an "information mule" in a cocaine ring. When the organization was busted, the transporters, dealers, and organizers pled down to various lower sentences, but Ms. Johnson received the maximum sentence, according to a strict interpretation of the law: life plus 25 years.

In prison, she returned to the faith of her childhood, sought education, and encouraged other inmates through theatrical performances and Bible studies. When President Obama reformed mandatory sentencing guidelines in an effort to achieve more fairness in the system, he granted clemency to a record 231 non-violent offenders in a single day. Alice Marie Johnson was not one of them, even though he was aware of her case. Still, she held on to her faith and to hope. When President Trump took office, celebrity Kim Kardashian pled Ms. Johnson's case directly to him. In June of 2018, she was released from prison after 21 years behind bars.

Her case illustrates the importance of fairness. When I interviewed her for television in 2019, she admitted her guilt in the case while expressing gratitude to those who lobbied on her behalf. The bottom line is that she deserved punishment, but her sentence was blatantly unfair. Yes, it was legal. Yes, it was according to established criminal guidelines. But no, it was not fair. It was her first offense, she didn't directly handle or distribute narcotics, and she did not organize the criminal activity. The people who played more active roles received lesser sentences. She was a bit player. She deserved a punishment that fit the crime.

God is interested in fairness. "The Lord demands accurate scales and balances; he sets the standards for fairness" (Proverbs 16:11 NLT). If you're looking for the best definition of fairness, the answer is "God." How does that translate to our lives? It can be summed up in a few qualities.

First, honesty. We must have some recognition of truth in order to deal fairly. That's why "identifying" as a girl to compete in girls' athletics fails the test—it's not honest. Boys inherently develop more muscle, enabling them to run faster, jump higher, and grow stronger. Sure, you can find a girl who can beat a boy in a head-to-head match, but overall boys will outperform girls in any athletic arena. If we're honest about gender, then it's only fair that we compete as such.

In everyday life, this can be seen in various ways. People are naturally gifted in different areas. Some work harder than others. The person who excels on the job should be rewarded accordingly. The salesperson who has knowledge of the item or service being sold and hustles to close deals should make more money than those who sell less. The person who takes on more responsibility should receive more than the one who just shows up, does what is required, and goes home at the end of the day.

My four children all did well in school, but they did not all achieve the same grades. As parents, we recognized their differences and held them to standards according to their abilities. If they worked hard, met the requirements, and gave their best, we did not worry about the actual grades. Two of them earned straight A's, while the other two did well with B's and the occasional C. We did not treat them with a strict equality, but with an honest fairness.

Second, justice. God is a big fan of justice. "Justice is a joy to the godly, but it terrifies evildoers" (Proverbs 21:15 NLT). The essence of this concept is that when a conflict occurs, the case must be decided. When someone commits murder, the case must be decided fairly. When children rebel against their parents, their case must be decided fairly. When a person cheats another, again, the case must be decided fairly. When any act of harm is committed, it is unjust for it to go undecided. Since God is the ultimate standard for fairness, humans must attempt to emulate His standard.

That standard under the Old Testament was harsh. Murderers, rebels, and swindlers could be punished severely, often with death. It is interesting, however, to note that as tough as the ancient law was, it removed from the victim the power to pass judgment and execute a sentence. It put it in a court of law. The relative of a murder victim could not hunt down and kill the perpetrator. An individual could not extract restitution directly from a thief. A parent could no longer condemn a child to death. Only an impartial, emotionally detached court held the authority to carry out justice.

We see this in civilized societies today. If someone wrongs you, you are not allowed to gather your cousins and administer vigilante justice with baseball bats. That's only for the movies. Therefore, the pursuit of fair judgment is a societal one. Christians must be dedicated to fairness in civil justice. In American history, the gap between justice for whites and blacks has, at times, been shamefully wide. Equal treatment before the law is not only fair, it is a God-given mandate.

On an individual level, we see the third characteristic of fairness, which is grace. God is the author of ultimate grace in that we are offered a complete pardon of all of our sins against God through the atonement of Jesus Christ. Our sin demands spiritual death, yet we are freely presented with eternal life, if we will put our faith in Christ. This allows us to offer overwhelming grace on an individual level while maintaining justice on a civil level.

To illustrate this, consider the case of Botham Jean. On September 6, 2018, Jean was sitting in his apartment eating ice cream and watching television when Dallas Police Officer Amber Guyger opened the door and shot him dead. The two had never met and Officer Guyger claimed she accidentally entered the wrong apartment and, thinking it was her own, assumed him to be a burglar. In an emotional trial, she was convicted of murder. After sentencing, Jean's family was given the opportunity to address Guyger. Botham's brother, Brandt, surprised everyone by proclaiming forgiveness for his brother's killer. He then gained permission from the judge to hug Guyger and urged her to give her life to Christ.

Here we see both grace and justice working together. Brandt demonstrated amazing, liberating grace even as the government executed justice by sending her to prison. This is the balance that enables fairness.

As you consider how to implement fairness in your dealings with people, integrate honesty, justice, and grace as needed. Don't hide misdeeds that need to come to light, but do not seek to be an instrument of destruction. Allow governing authorities to administer punishment as warranted but strive for a fair system of justice while expressing personal grace for the redemption of souls.

DAY 6
Do the Right Thing

On January 7, 2015, Corrine Rey faced a horrifying moral dilemma with only seconds to respond. She worked as a cartoonist at the satirical magazine *Charlie Hebdo* in Paris, France. She left the office to pick up her daughter from kindergarten. When she returned, two gunmen met her at the door, threatening to shoot her daughter if she refused to enter the entry code of the door. She complied. The Jihadists went inside and began shooting, killing 12 people and injuring 11 others. Corrine and her daughter were unharmed.

Many things are clearly wrong or right. Murder, theft, and adultery are always wrong. Defending the weak, helping the oppressed, and expressing love are always right. Other things are not always as clear-cut. Most of us will never face the life-and-death situation that Corrine Rey experienced, but we do find ourselves in situations where right and wrong are not obvious. If you pay for a five-dollar cup of coffee with a ten-dollar bill, but the cashier gives you fifteen in return, thinking you paid with a twenty-dollar bill, do you keep it or give it back? Do you lie to prevent hurting someone? If a co-worker has an addiction, do you confront him or her privately, do you tell your boss, or do you say nothing? If a loved one is suffering from a terminal illness, do you allow them to refuse life-prolonging medical care or force them to endure it?

We face choices of varying degrees every day. Relying on our own innate goodness or opinion of right and wrong creates a society with a billion different definitions of right and wrong. We need a higher authority than ourselves. Society provides a level of acceptable morality, but it is frightfully tenuous. What is right one day can be wrong the next. In many cases what is socially "right" is morally wrong.

Nazi Germany is an obvious example from modern history. Early on, disdain for Jews was not only allowed, it was encouraged. It was, according to society, the "right" attitude. This led to abuse and eventually genocide. Contemporary examples exist as well. Oppression of women is the norm in many countries in the Middle East. Prostitution is condoned in parts of Europe and Asia. In America, and most Western countries, "no fault" divorce doesn't even raise an eyebrow, and abortion is celebrated.

Governments face inherent limits. In practical terms, it's impossible to have a free people when everything that is morally wrong is outlawed. While we criminalize "hate crimes," we cannot punish hate-filled people until they act out in certain ways.

If you are looking for a stable, authentic source to determine right and wrong, you must look beyond yourself, society, or the government. You must look to the perfect standard, which is God. If you want to do what is right, you must look to Him for direction. This requires a realization that God is, at His core, the essence of goodness. If He were some sort of arbitrary, narcissistic Roman-style god, then there would be no reliable standard of goodness, allowing each of us to create our own definition or right and wrong or, as has been the case throughout history, enabling societies to agree upon or randomly impose standards of acceptable behavior, as in the case of Nazi Germany. Other countries may condemn a society's values, but what justification do they have if right and wrong are arbitrary? There must be a rock-solid, never-changing foundation. There is none other than the God of the Bible.

We tend to have an odd view of God as one who makes irrational demands that we can never follow or think that He is an often angry supreme being who must be appeased by keeping a set of rules. But if He is both good and perfect, then following His ways is the path to goodness and perfection. His nature reveals right and wrong. In a world full of evil, pain, and brokenness, God's ways are not legalistic edicts under which we must suffer, but they are the secret to a life of fulfillment and wholeness. To use a limited analogy, His rules are more like a coach instructing a player on how to be the best player he or she can be. When we follow them, we become better and happier.

"There is a path before each person that seems right, but it ends in death" (Proverbs 14:12 NLT). Press that idea up against Jesus' claims that "I came that they may have life, and have it abundantly" (John 10:10b NASB) and "If you love Me, you will keep My commandments" (John 14:15 NASB). Jesus came to rescue us from our own definition of right and wrong because it kills us. He wants us to live. Obedience is not an act of punishment, even when it requires denying our own will, but a step in the direction of a better life. It may feel like we're giving up something because our will often defies Him like a petulant child resists the guidance of a loving parent. But "The Lord is more pleased when we do what is right and just than when we offer him sacrifices" (Proverbs 21:3 NLT). Accepting and living according to His definition of right and wrong does more for us than it does Him. It leads to the life He wants to give us, which pleases Him because He is a good and loving Father.

When we face simple daily choices, or even complex moral dilemmas, we must look to God's character and seek His guidance in order to respond rightly. We won't be perfect—He understands that—but by seeking to do right in every situation, we are perfected.

When you do make a mistake, admit it, make amends as much as possible, and move on. You will stumble on your path, but fall forward as you strive to do right. Get back up, learn from your mistakes, and keep improving.

DAY 7
Be Hateful

Yes, you read that right. Performing better works in your life and in the lives of those you love requires a certain hatred. We think of love and hate as opposites because they move in opposing directions. But if you think about it, they are both just strong feelings related to something or someone you care about. Love cares in a way that wants to build up. Hate cares in a way that wants to destroy. They seek completely different outcomes. Yet the absence of one does not indicate the presence of the other. In other words, the fact that you don't hate something does not mean that you love it.

I would argue that the alternative to love is not hate, but indifference. Love cares; indifference does not. Love wants something constructive to happen. Hate wants something destructive to happen. Indifference wants nothing. You can feel love and hate at the same time, but you cannot feel either while feeling indifferent. That's why you can love someone who has a life-threatening disease while hating the disease. You care very much that the person gets well, so you take him or her to the doctor for treatment that will destroy the disease. If you didn't care about the person or the sickness, you would do nothing, and the disease would take its course. But because you love the person and, at the same time, hate the threat to his or her life, you do something.

The alternative to hatred is tolerance. This can be good or bad, depending on the context. Take sex trafficking. The person who hates the abuse and enslavement of women will work to destroy it by condemning it, exposing it, and taking direct action to prevent and eradicate it. Those who turn a blind eye of indifference may not *like* sex trafficking, but they don't *hate* it. The one who truly hates, in the sense of desiring its destruction, will work to destroy it. Because of a passionate intolerance for sex trafficking, that person is motivated to action. This is a proper expression of hatred. The alternative is not necessarily "loving" sex trafficking, but simply tolerating it. Silence becomes assent.

Many good works are not motivated solely by love, but also by hate. A man who hates judicial injustice will work to overturn those falsely sentenced. He may never know or care specifically about the inmate, but his intolerance of wrongful incarceration compels him to seek the release of strangers. A woman who hates hunger volunteers at a local food bank not because she knows every hungry person in her city, but because she refuses to give in to the idea that a child should go through a day without a meal.

Hatred can be a powerful, positive motivator when it is focused on those things that hurt people. Conversely, hatred is terribly destructive when focused on people themselves. This is why we must learn what to hate. Notice I said *what*, not *who*. Healthy hatred (yes, there is such a thing) is an intolerance for wrong attitudes and actions. Even when embodied in people, a proper hatred will not seek the destruction of the person holding to a wrong attitude or action. Instead, it will seek to free the person from the diseased idea, thereby destroying the evil while redeeming the individual. Love and hate should actually work together.

I have seen this in action on the streets of cities worldwide. I admit that when I meet a sex trafficker, especially of underage girls, I feel a visceral reaction that is certainly not love. Understanding that my enemy is not the young man (or sometimes older woman) standing in front of me, but the horrible business of prostitution and enslavement, enables me to see the pimp as someone also enslaved (though not in an equal sense) by evil. Hatred for sex trafficking motivates intervention, but love for all people—both the oppressed and the oppressors—opens the door to redemption for everyone involved. I have seen pimps transformed in their thinking. They often become the most effective warriors against sex trafficking. This is a real and significant victory because it destroys what is wicked while rescuing people from the wickedness.

Properly directed hatred starts with self-examination. Do you tolerate dishonesty in your own life? Do you dismiss your own arrogance? Are you frequently mean to others? Until you passionately care about your own attitudes, hating the negative ones, you will allow them to continue. Learning to hate, and therefore not tolerate, the darkness in your own heart will motivate you to live in the light.

Mastering this within yourself guides you to better confront it in others. When you see things in other people that you know are destructive, you don't have to tolerate them. If, for example, a loved one is consumed with bitterness, you must first recognize it, then hold an inner intolerance to the damage that bitterness seeks to do. Simultaneously, you can work to eradicate it, thereby helping your loved one. This "love the sinner, hate the sin" approach is the only practical and effective way to combat the deadly attitudes that people hold. If we truly love the person, we won't be indifferent to their cancerous thoughts. When we properly hate their ideas, we will be motivated to do all that we can to eradicate them. In doing so, we cure them of their terminal thinking. This is hate that knows how to love, and that is good hate.

WEEK 7

"There is only one corner of the universe you can be certain of improving, and that's your own self."

—ALDOUS HUXLEY

UPGRADE
Your Self

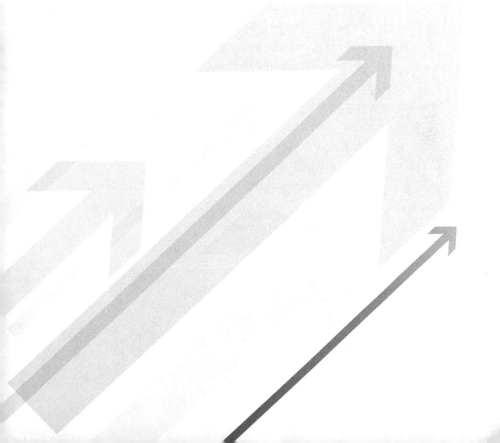

Self-help books are sometimes mocked in religious circles, and there can be good reason to do so. Vanity is foolishness. Self-centeredness is repulsive. Jesus said, "If any of you wants to be my follower, you must give up your own way, take up your cross, and follow me. If you try to hang on to your life, you will lose it. But if you give up your life for my sake, you will save it" (Matthew 16:24-25 NLT).

Notice that there are two parts to the act of self-denial: giving up your own way of life and saving it. Real self-help accomplishes both. It's the process of shaping yourself in the way God designed, not the way that comes naturally to mankind's sinful nature. Your best self is one conformed to the image of Christ, not the one who gets everything you think you need.

In this context, there is a "better self" to be had. Pursuing this self is good because it is one molded by our Creator. By viewing ourselves as ones created to emulate, honor, and reflect the One who made us in His image, gave us new life and declared us "new creations," and renews our minds daily, we can follow His guidelines for the ultimate upgrade.

DAY 1
Build Your Reputation

A strange new industry has arisen in the age of the internet. It's called "online reputation management." Companies that do this peddle services like "the permanent deletion of negative online material," "fixing your online reputation," and "inoculating your vulnerability." I have no idea what that last one means, but the general idea is that when someone says something negative about you or your company, these people try to get rid of it, usually by deleting it. Apparently, a reputation is a fickle thing, at least online.

Most people realize that the internet brings out the best and worst of people. Anyone can say anything. Truth and fiction require more than a link or a comment. Real life is more concrete. Reputations are not fabricated as easily as an Instagram post. The way people think of you comes directly from their interactions with you. If your name is mentioned when you are not around, what do people say and think?

Your reputation rightly comes from the pattern of characteristics in your life. If you have a reputation as being kind, it's because many people have witnessed your kindness. If you have a reputation for being late, it's because many people have waited on you. Your words and actions create impressions, either good or bad. We can never fully control what other people think, but if we speak and act with purpose and authenticity, we can earn a positive image *offline*, as in "the real world."

"Choose a good reputation over great riches; being held in high esteem is better than silver or gold" (Proverbs 22:1 NLT). Money can buy search engine rankings, but it can't buy a life characterized by love, honor, respect, kindness, patience, and every other positive attribute. Yet it is far more valuable than a million dollars or a million followers.

A friend of mine was treated poorly at his job. He worked hard and sought to be an asset to the organization, but his boss was less than gracious. Eventually, he left. His boss took it as personal betrayal. Some in the organization spoke ill of my friend, but he never fired back. Not once. Instead, he praised the organization and refused to badmouth anyone there, even when it was warranted. Years later, their attitudes toward him had completely turned around. His consistency and self-control built a good reputation for him, and it paid off.

"Never let loyalty and kindness leave you! Tie them around your neck as a reminder. Write them deep within your heart. Then you will find favor with both God and people, and you will earn a good reputation" (Proverbs 3:3-4 NLT). Within this pearl of wisdom, we find two key elements of a good reputation: loyalty and kindness.

When my friend left his job, he stayed loyal—not necessarily to his former boss (though he always treated him with respect) but to his professed beliefs as a Christian and to God. Loyalty doesn't mean staying in a bad situation. It means staying true to the core teachings of Christ. This will lead to loyalty toward certain individuals, especially in non-occupational settings like friendships and family relationships. And it will ultimately reflect on our relationship with God. If loyalty to Christ's teachings conflicts with loyalty to a person, the choice is clear. Always go with God. Beyond that, stay consistently gracious, even when people don't deserve it, and you will earn a good reputation.

Second, maintain kindness, even in the face of others' bad behavior. Don't repay evil for evil. When people insult you, don't retaliate with more insults. Instead, pay them back with a blessing. That's easy to say, but very hard to do. When you find yourself in that situation, remember this: God has called you to react that way and when you do, He will bless you. That's a promise straight from 1 Peter 3:9.

At some point, you will find yourself in a similar position as my friend. That's a guarantee. People will insult you, hurt you, and mistreat you. They will be wrong, hurtful, or just plain mean. They will deserve to be put in their place. You will then have two choices: receive God's blessing or give them what they deserve. Which do you really want? Do you prefer to get even with a rotten person or get God's attention? If you respond with kindness, you are effectively saying, "God, I choose your way. Now I await your promised blessing!" When you look at it that way, which is the biblical way to look at it, choosing kindness is much easier. You can actually thank God for the opportunity. (It will also seriously mess with other people's heads, which is a small reward of its own!)

Those two powerful responses—kindness and loyalty—are the tools that forge a good reputation for yourself. Use them. Every word you say and everything you do builds your reputation, so why not make it a good one? Move beyond the short-sightedness of daily situations and play the long game. Plan now for your righteous response to people who harm you. That way, you'll never need to hire those "reputation managers." You'll be the master of your own good name.

DAY 2
Don't Suck Up

Nobody likes that person who "sucks up" to others with lavish compliments, all while working some personal angle. Nor do we enjoy being around someone who constantly and purposely tears down others. Those are two ditches on the side of the road in which you can easily wreck yourself if you're not careful. Learning the nuances of compliments and criticism makes all the difference in the world—keeping you centered, safe, and cruising to a better self.

When we genuinely appreciate something positive about someone and express it, that's called a compliment. "Great shot," "nice outfit," or "good idea" are common compliments. These are positive, simple encouragements to build others up in a healthy way when genuinely intentional. But when personal angles come into play, they go from compliment to flattery. Flattery is a give-to-get transaction. We say something nice because we want something from that person. It's no longer *building* someone up, but rather *setting* someone up.

"To flatter friends is to lay a trap for their feet" (Proverbs 29:5 NLT). This is so not cool. If you routinely do this, you will find your friendships don't last very long. Flattery ruins relationships. As soon as others grow wise to your motives, they will distance themselves from you—and rightly so. Nobody likes being manipulated. It they are so emotionally stunted that they can't separate from you, the relationship is bound for abuse, with you as the abuser. If you don't have a sincere compliment to offer with no expectation of something in return, stay silent.

When you do see an opportunity for a compliment, learn the art of timing. Sometimes genuine praise can look like sucking up. If your boss has a great idea in a meeting, maybe send an email later rather than paying tribute in front of everyone. Also, consider the appropriateness of it. For example, married men dishing out compliments to women about their appearance can quickly turn lecherous or creepy. Even if innocent, it can leave people speculating. Compliments are a little like bricks: They can be used to build wonderful things, but if hurled recklessly, they can do a lot of damage. Learn to carefully and purposely place them where they accomplish what they should.

The other easy mistake is destructive criticism. Though it is not always obvious, it too has a selfish motive at heart.

Before we delve into this, I need to address the problem with the English language inherent in this term. Criticism has two different definitions. One automatically assumes disapproval. It bears a constant cynicism. The other merely analyzes and evaluates, pointing out positives and negatives for the sake of awareness. For clarity, I'll use the modifiers "destructive" and "constructive" to distinguish between the two.

Destructive criticism seeks only to tear down others. It finds the crack in every plan and calls it a chasm. It does not merely point out problems or imperfections, it mocks them. It swings analysis as a club, weaponizing every conversation. It might admit to some good, but it always sees the bad as bigger. Though it is too proud or cowardly to admit it, destructive criticism seeks to raise itself up by destroying everyone else.

On the other hand, constructive criticism maintains honesty, seeing potential problems, flaws, and pitfalls while seeking a way to remedy them. It analyzes to make something stronger, not weaker. It acknowledges the bad but finds the good and builds on it. It leaves room for others to take credit and allows everyone to win.

The practical implementation of constructive criticism requires self-awareness, consideration of others, and a certain art in communication. You must hear yourself and understand how others hear you. You must purposely put their interests over your own. And you have to learn how to choose your words and tone so that they work toward a positive outcome. Destructive criticism will seek to destroy a person or idea. Constructive criticism will seek to improve them, even when it means changing tack or starting over.

For example, if someone presents a plan or idea that is not sound, the easiest thing to do is smash it to pieces. Constructive criticism will politely test it. Questions are a good starting point. "Where do you see that taking us in a year?" "How will you deal with this potential problem?" That sort of thing. Lead someone to your conclusion; don't embarrass them with it. Let people down easily. Even when it's necessary to cut a leg out from underneath something or someone, leave one to stand on.

Trust is an essential element in the effective use of constructive criticism. Sometimes, you are not in the position to offer criticism because you don't have a strong enough relationship with others. In that case, be very careful or very quiet. When you do offer it, be simultaneously honest, gentle, and kind. "The heartfelt counsel of a friend is as sweet as perfume and incense" (Proverbs 27:9 NLT). When someone truly understands that you are trying to help them, even when offering criticism, it will be refreshing to them. Relationships with this healthy dynamic are perhaps the most valuable you can have in your life. Cultivate them in both directions—you helping them, and them helping you. If you can't take criticism, even the constructive kind, you have no business offering it to others.

"In the end, people appreciate honest criticism far more than flattery" (Proverbs 28:23 NLT). Learn how to set your self-interest aside and seek to build others up. Genuine concern and help without manipulation or meanness is refreshing. Mastering these skills will make you a reliable friend, successful worker, and valuable asset in every circumstance.

DAY 3
Sleep Well

Have you ever lost sleep because something was not right in your life? Tossing and turning in bed while your mind tosses and turns is a miserable state. Lies demand constant plotting to avoid getting caught. Anger boils as your imagination carries out confrontation or revenge. Fear won't let you relax, wearing you down as time goes by. Worry envisions things that could happen, even when they haven't.

The word *integrity* comes from the same root as *integer*, which is a "whole number" or "complete unit." An integer is not a fraction. It is not divided. In the same way, a person with integrity is one who lives a singular, undivided life. It is distinguished by *wholeness*.

We all play different roles in different settings that dictate our behavior to a degree. If I'm leading the worship band or in charge of a television shoot, I'm pushing people along, giving instructions, and making sure we meet our goals. If I'm the background singer or camera operator, I'm following the lead of someone else, so I'm not stepping on his or her toes by trying to take charge. That's knowing one's role and fulfilling it. Either way, I'm the same person in the way I treat people and the characteristics I try to live by, like honesty, respect, patience, and so on.

However, when we become entirely different people in different settings, we expose our fractured spirit. To use an extreme, yet obvious, example, consider the priest who led mass, presiding over communion and speaking blessings on parishioners, then molested altar boys in the same week. Most people would simply label that man as evil, and certainly the sexual abuse of any person, especially a child, is nothing but evil. But the reality is that many priests caught in such vile behavior also displayed wonderful characteristics for years, serving others with compassion and teaching Godly principles. That's why the revelations of abuse caused so much shock and confusion. If everyone thought the abusers were nothing but evil men their whole lives, there would have been no surprise. But the fact that they were divided men—good in most settings but hiding a terrible crime—enabled denial and cover-up for a long time, then stunned people who only knew the "good" priest when the truth came out.

This is a clear example of a lack of integrity—divided men leading fractured lives. Imagine them reading in Proverbs, "People with integrity walk safely, but those who follow crooked paths will be exposed" (10:9 NLT). I don't know how any of them ever got a good night's sleep. I suspect that most never did, unless they were complete psychopaths lacking any empathy. I can guarantee that if they were truly born again, they were living in their own hell, tortured by their temptation-turned-sin. Their secrets destroyed many lives, and their exposure destroyed even more.

At the end of the last century, the energy company Enron had quickly built a reputation as an innovative corporation, leading the way in the emerging tech field while enjoying the traditional stability of an established sector. They built power plants and managed gas lines while creating new, internet-friendly commodities like weather futures and bandwidth. The company peaked at a value of about $70 billion and employed thousands. The problem: Executives lied about the company's income and used shell companies and shady accounting to hide massive debt. You know these guys were losing sleep at night!

When things started unraveling, the company's stock value plummeted. Thousands lost jobs, and tens of thousands of former employees lost all or part of their retirement. When the company finally filed bankruptcy, another 5,600 Enron employees lost their jobs. It was the biggest bankruptcy in U.S. history at the time. After months of investigations, 24 Enron executives were convicted and several went to prison, including top executives. The Enron collapse also took down the respected accounting firm Arthur Andersen.[22,23,24] The lack of integrity by a few key people impacted thousands, causing pain and hardship for decades.

Most of us battle wholeness on a lesser level, but it's still hugely important to confront. Being a nice guy at work but a jerk to your wife demonstrates a destructive division in your character. Putting on a smile in front of your peers while verbally savaging them behind their backs says more about your lack of integrity than it does their faults. We must seek wholeness for the sake of wholeness. External expressions only occur when there is internal fracture. Spotting them in others protects us from being caught in their inevitable downfall. Spotting it in ourselves allows us time to mend the faults before falling apart.

Perhaps one can find some wholeness through self-examination, psychological counseling, or other non-Christian methods; but I am convinced the only way to repair a broken person is to take him or her to our Maker. Paul calls those who have been spiritually reborn in Christ a "new person" (see 2 Corinthians 5:17) and "God's masterpiece" (see Ephesians 2:10). James explains how we can be "perfect and complete, needing nothing" (see James 1:2-4). Jesus told his followers to "be perfect, even as your Father in heaven is perfect" (see Matthew 5:48). The connotation in Jesus' statement is about wholeness. It comes at the end of his teaching on loving your enemies and being kind to those are not kind to us, which does not come naturally. True integrity, I believe, only comes when we allow God to work in us to heal the fractures and bridge the divides.

Here's the exciting news when we live with integrity: God notices, and He really likes it. "The Lord detests people with crooked hearts, but he delights in those with integrity" (Proverbs 11:20 NLT). Maybe your parents took delight in your achievements as a child. Perhaps your mother or father noticed the good things you did. Or it could be that you felt overlooked and underappreciated (and still do). Either way, when you live a life of integrity, God sees you. And He *delights* in you.

When you live with the same character in private and in public, pursuing and demonstrating a wholeness in every area of your life, and delighting the very Creator of the universe, you fulfill one of the most important purposes in your life. Others will like you better and you will, too.

DAY 4
Don't Be Impressed with Yourself

I have made enough mistakes in my life that when I do things right, it is more of a relief than anything. But apparently there are some people who do everything right all the time. You know the type— gifted, smart, athletic, good-looking, rich . . . whatever. Frankly, I've never understood it. You may be great at something, and I applaud you for it. But I know you have shortcomings. We all do!

Still, falling into a bit of pride is easy—even for those of us who are aware of our faults. We string together a few victories and start to feel like perpetual champions. So here's the warning, as the subheading states: Don't be impressed with yourself. Enjoy your wins. Celebrate them when appropriate. But know that everyone has ups and downs. Your victory is great. I rejoice with you. Just maintain an attitude of gratefulness for your wins. As soon as you get cocky about it, I'm out. Of course, that may mean nothing to you, but here's something that should get your attention: As soon as you fill up with pride, God is out too. He really doesn't like it. In fact, He hates it. So much so that He makes a few promises for those consumed by pride.

First, you will get knocked down (see Proverbs 29:23).

I'm not much of a rodeo kind of guy, but I've lived most of my life in Texas, so I've seen a few. The most exciting event is bull riding. The very best bull riders go eight seconds on a bucking beast that weighs around 2,000 pounds. Eight seconds! Imagine trying to ride one of those things for a minute or an hour. It can't be done. Like a cowboy trying to eternally stay atop bucking bull, pride takes a seat that is impossible to maintain. It will eventually throw you harder than the meanest bovine, and the landing will be very painful. You might even get gored.

Second, God will oppose you (see James 4:6).

If you are ever at the beach and decide to swim in the ocean, here's a tip: If you find yourself being swept away from shore by a riptide, don't try to fight it. Swim parallel to the beach until you're out of the rip, then swim to shore. You can't fight a riptide. Here's another tip: You have a far better chance fighting a riptide than fighting God. There is no getting away from Him. You can't "swim" far enough or fast enough. If you are in opposition to Him, you will find yourself exhausted and in way over your head.

Third, He will allow you to be disgraced because of it
(see Proverbs 11:2).

I admit it. I've totally covered things up before, especially as a teen-ager. Why? I didn't want my parents to find out. They always did anyway, but that instinct to run and hide is as old as Adam in the garden with the fig leaves. Nobody likes to feel naked and exposed. Well, not normal people, but I digress. When we confess our sins, God promises to forgive them and put us back together. When we have so much pride that we think we can hide them from Him, He promises to expose them. Given this truth, it is obvious that pride not only makes people annoying but also stupid. I mean, seriously, who thinks they can hide something from an all-knowing, all-seeing God? Sure, you can deny God's existence and exempt yourself from thinking your pride won't lead to disgrace, but it will anyway. You don't have to believe in gravity, but you'll hit the ground just as hard as everyone else. If you know you're harboring pride and you do believe in God, get ahead of the disgrace and confess it. Go to battle. As long as you're fighting against pride, you haven't lost, so don't wait for humiliation and scandal. It might be painful to admit your pride now, but it will be misery on a whole new level if you hang onto it.

Fourth, He will punish it (see Proverbs 16:5).

An early American settler heading to California stopped in southern Montana during early summer. *This land is perfect*, he thought. And it was . . . in June. A seasoned explorer passed him in July and said, "You'll want to move on. Winter will come, and it will be cold." The settler looked around and said, "I've been here a while, and it has only gotten better." The explorer shook his head and said, "It's fine now, but when the snow comes, you won't survive." The settler ignored him and enjoyed the rest of the summer and beauty of the fall. In January, he froze to death in his cabin.

Maybe you're thinking, *I know some prideful people who haven't been punished.* You're right. God is patient. Far more than most humans. He doesn't want you to feel the wrath that pride naturally brings on itself. He wants to purge it so you can be free from suffering. In time, however, the seasons will change and you won't survive. Don't be that guy.

That's the bad news. Now the good news. If you will humble yourself instead of waiting to be humbled, God will lift you up (see James 4:10; 1 Peter 5:6). There's no middle ground there. Either God will humble you or He will lift you up. Which sounds better?

When you dig into the metaphorical meaning of the promise to "lift up" or "exalt," it gets even better. There are two uses: to raise to the very summit of opulence and prosperity; and to exalt, to raise to dignity, honor, and happiness. In addition, humility brings wisdom, forgiveness, healing, and direction (see Proverbs 11:2; 2 Chronicles 7:14; Psalm 25:9). If the negative destination of pride doesn't motivate you to run from it, the positive promises surely have to stir up a desire to shed it. Check out that list again: opulence, prosperity, dignity, honor, and happiness. Now compare it to the alternatives: getting knocked down, being opposed by God, being disgraced, and facing punishment. Once you grasp this truth, you will rush to humble yourself.

How do you go about getting rid of pride? There are some pro-active measures you can take, in addition to admitting that you struggle with it. First, practice patience. Pride is inherently impatient. When you feel it rising up in you, take control of it, and force yourself to be patient. When you feel yourself gritting your teeth, ask God for help. Quote Scripture. Count to 10. Do whatever it takes. This develops humility. Second, spend time with those you tend to look down on. Seek them out. Search for value in them. Meet their needs. Hear their hearts. This takes the focus off yourself and develops compassion. Third, look for opportunities to express kindness. When you are full of pride, your focus is on yourself. When you actively seek ways to show kindness to others, you are forced to think less about yourself and more about others. These are biblical therapies designed to cure your pride.

Pride really is one of your biggest enemies. Humility may not seem like a natural path to happiness, but once you comprehend the beauty of it, you will learn to love it. Along the way, you will discover that others appreciate the qualities that stem from true humility, and you will be more content and at peace with yourself.

DAY 5
Stay Sober

Sobriety is usually associated with drugs and alcohol. Certainly, an environment of addiction or drunkenness creates its own chaos and if that's an area of struggle, make it a priority to get help. But sobriety also applies to our way of thinking. Sober thinking is sensible, sound, and clear-headed. Good thoughts are those that align with sound values and ideas.

Most self-induced problems arise from two things: our words and our actions. Yet those are merely symptomatic of our thoughts. What we think expresses itself through what we do and say. What we do and say determines the environment around us. A healthy *you* starts in the mind.

Sober thinking has purpose. Just as a house is built on a strong foundation with a carefully designed framework, a home must have good footing and a plan to succeed. What do you want for your household? Security, affection, and communication have to be established. Creating an environment for emotionally and spiritually healthy families does not come without effort. The example you set will impact those closest to you, and it starts with clear thinking.

A friend of mine on the worship team at our church began participating less and less. I caught him one day and asked about his absence. He had two young sons and coached their baseball team, which had been traveling and playing in weekend tournaments, so giving up both Saturday and Sunday to volunteer singing was impossible, he claimed. I understood. It can be difficult and taxing to work a full week on the job, spend time with your children in all of their activities, and volunteer several hours on the weekend. I applauded his commitment to his family. Months later, I heard that he was leaving his wife and sons for a woman he had met at work.

I wondered, *What is he thinking?* We weren't that close, but close enough that he could have talked to me about marriage difficulties, and I would have listened and encouraged him in the right way. I certainly would not have suggested he blow up his family to pursue his own selfish pleasure. He probably knew that, which would explain why he wouldn't answer my phone calls. I don't really know what happened. What I do know is that his thought process was royally screwed up. His thinking was as clouded as a lap-legged drunk. Otherwise he would have seen the damage he was doing to the three closest people in his life.

His mind was under the influence of a desire for a woman not his wife and a selfishness that blinded him to the intense pain he caused his bride and the long-term struggle he would be placing on two innocent boys. I haven't heard from him or seen him since.

A sober person does things that make sense. Someone under the influence of ungodly thoughts and emotions does things that make no sense at all. Lust breaks up a family. Rage physically abuses a woman. Addiction forfeits an inheritance. Greed destroys a friendship. Envy sows discontent. Bitterness drives people apart. The litany of thoughts and emotions that lead to destruction demonstrate how nonsensical they are. Ask any newlywed, "Do you want to scar your spouse for life and ensure your children need therapy through adulthood?" He or she will look at you like you're an idiot; yet give it 5, 10, or 20 years and too many of them will have done just that. It is insane. And it's the result of a mind clouded by toxicity.

There are three hallmarks of physical intoxication that parallel what happens when our thoughts are under a bad influence.

First, a drunk person has tunnel vision. He doesn't see much to the right or left and has zero awareness of what's behind him. In fact, he can hardly focus on the thing he's looking at. He has a hard time finding his way because he doesn't pick up on the landmarks and signs that he normally would when sober. He stumbles over everything, both big and small.

When our minds are under the influence of toxic thoughts and emotions, we lose sight of our vision in life. We no longer focus on our goals and miss the signs that let us know we are off track. We are knocked off balance by things hitting us from every side. Unseen things overtake us from behind, seemingly out of nowhere. Everything causes us to stumble—even the little things.

Second, a drunk person is slow to react. Processing a situation takes longer, and responding to it requires more effort than usual. He doesn't spot threats quickly. If he is driving, he is a danger to himself and everyone he encounters.

When we're not clear-headed, we don't know how to properly handle situations. Simple ones become complicated, and difficult ones become impossible. It's exhausting just getting through the day. Others see problems headed our way, but we don't anticipate it and head straight into trouble. If we're in charge, it's dangerous for everyone close to us.

Third, a drunk person has poor judgment. He does things inconsistent with his usual character. Bad ideas seem okay. He takes stupid risks. He acts without thinking.

Sober thinking analyzes situations, weighs the options, seeks constructive input, and takes the most reasonable course of action. We don't rush into things, respond rashly, or get blindsided by consequences. We make mistakes, but we learn from them. Our judgment may not be perfect, but it improves with experience and learns to mitigate risk.

If you want a strong, happy family, you need clear vision, proper responses, and sound judgment. It is not a state of perfection, but a process of perfecting. We grow together through experiences, cling to each other in the hard times, and pursue the best for every individual. This is the ideal family for most people, even when not the reality. That's why we need to be our sharpest mentally and spiritually to maintain the vision. We won't always fulfill our hopes or meet our expectations, but we can keep our goals in sight, clearly working to maintain the positive areas and improve the things that require work. This is sensible, sober thinking.

DAY 6
Remember Who's in Charge

There's an old bumper sticker that says, "God is my co-pilot." I'm sure whoever came up with that meant well, but it's terribly misguided because it implies that we are in the pilot seat, when the reality is that this arrangement is a recipe for disaster. If you want to fly off course, relegate God to your assistant while you take charge.

This subtly manifests itself when we make our own plans, then ask God to bless them. There is a difference between using our God-given gifts and desires for ourselves, even when inviting God to take part, and submitting our will completely to Him. Christ modeled this attitude in the Garden of Gethsemane as He expressed His desire with the caveat, "Not my will, but Yours." God wants to hear our ideas, dreams, and ambitions. He invites it. But He also knows what is best for us, so we are wise to lay them out, then lay them down. He sees down the road much farther than we possibly can.

If you have children, you know what it's like at Christmas. A child's wish list ranges from cute to ludicrous. Even the most mature, serious child can wish for something that, as a parent, you know is a bad idea. God is a perfect Father who wants to give us good gifts, but His sense of "good" is far superior to ours. We should make our wishes known, then acknowledge and accept His judgment.

He has given us direction when it comes to making our plans. He says that if we want our plans to succeed, we should commit our daily actions to Him. That means the small things. If you have a job, do it as if it's your highest calling. If you are raising children, treat them as your personal mission field. View those around you—work, school, church, neighborhood, sports teams, clubs—as the ones God has put in your path for you to love, encourage, help, pray for, and show His attributes. That's God's design for every believer's life, so you are guaranteed success when you follow this plan.

If you don't particularly like your job, imagine the difference it would make if you woke up every morning praying, "Lord, help me to show You to my co-workers today." If that's your mission, the workday becomes much more interesting, and the irritations seem less significant. Sure, you may have a boss at the workplace, but when you are ultimately working for God, your attitude drastically changes. Now a job that may not fit your career plan suddenly becomes a part of God's plan, which promises success on a whole new level.

Frustration comes when we fail to recognize and prioritize God's plans. We can make our own plans, but only God's will prevail. We can set goals such as a high-paying job, a distinguished family, a recognized name, or whatever. The question is not whose plans will succeed. That's already determined. The question is whether you will accept the invitation to be a part of God's success or waste time pursuing your own goals. When we put Him in the pilot seat and fly with Him, we will arrive at a destination better than we can imagine. When we pilot our own lives, the most likely result is a disastrous crash.

Staying close to God's purpose and plan sets us on a course guaranteed to find fulfillment. His name is described in Proverbs as a "strong fortress." That military analogy denotes several things, all of which are desirable and even necessary to make it through this life.

First, it's a place of safety. This is where you want to be during a time of war. Your enemies cannot get to you there. Life is filled with battles. We have internal struggles that threaten our peace. External forces come against us and our loved ones. The strongest soldier can only fight in the battlefield for so long. Eventually we all need a place of retreat, where the sanctuary of companions and impenetrability of the walls allow us to heal from wounds and rest from exertion. When you feel overwhelmed or your plans seem to fall apart, run to the fortress. (By the way, staying close to the fortress at all times makes it a short run.)

Second, a strong fortress is a fortified city. That means weapons. If you don't already know, you are not getting anywhere in life without a fight. We fight to stay focused on what is right. We fight to take every thought captive. We fight to protect those close to us. We fight for our marriages, families, communities, and nations. Sometimes we have to fight just to get out of bed each day! No sane person enters a fight without a weapon or two. Where do we get those weapons? Our fortified city, which is God. His weapons are not made of metal and gunpowder. His weapons are made of spirit and power, and they are strong enough to win every battle. But there's still a fight. Engagement is required. Grab your spiritual weapons, and you can participate in the victory. The outcome has already been decided, so why not?

Third, it's the most reliable place to be. A strong fortress is built on rocks, which provide a solid, immovable foundation. When you need rescued or deliverance from the perils of this world, take shelter in the place that cannot be shaken. In a world full of calamity and confusion, we desperately need a refuge that we know will always stand firm. Society's sense of right and wrong, good and bad, success and failure, and every other standard will continue to change with each generation, but God does not. We can count on His ways today, yesterday, and tomorrow. He is reliably the same, even as we go through different seasons of life, and He is always right. We can depend on Him through every situation.

God will prevail. If you want to experience His victory, stay under His command. Don't form your own rogue squadron and get into a dogfight, even if you think you're doing it on His behalf. He is in charge, so seek his leadership at all times. That way, you will be soaring like an ace in a winning war.

DAY 7
Trust God

Much of life comes down to one question: Do you trust God? It's easy to say "yes," but you will be tested. There will be things you don't understand, situations that don't make sense, and questions that go unanswered. The what, when, why, and how will not be found every time. The only certainty is the who.

The oldest book in the Bible is the book of Job. He was wealthy and blessed with a large family—a wife, seven sons, and three daughters. He was also a man described as "blameless, upright, fearing God and turning away from evil" (see Job 1:1). Even so, he suffered terribly. His children all died in one day. Natural disasters and attacks from enemies robbed him of his wealth. His health was ravaged by boils. His wife urged him to "curse God and die."

He would not.

He would, however, seeks answers and wrestle greatly with God. His friends tried to give him answers, but they fell short. Job could get no satisfactory answers for his what, when, why, and how, so he took his pain and confusion to the who.

God answered Job by putting him in his place. "Where were you when I laid the foundation of the earth?" God asked, asserting His omnipresence. "Have you ever in your life commanded the morning, and caused the dawn to know its place?" He asked, asserting his omnipotence. "Do you know the ordinances of the heavens, or fix their rule over the earth?" He asked, asserting His omniscience. God ends with the challenge, "Will the faultfinder contend with the Almighty?" (see Job 38-40).

Job acknowledged his humanity—his inability to grasp the universe, his powerlessness over most things, his limited knowledge and understanding, and his inherent inferiority to the Creator. "I know that You can do all things," he confessed to God, "and that no purpose of Yours can be thwarted." He admitted his own inadequacy by saying, "I have declared that which I did not understand." He submitted his will to God by saying, "I will ask You, and You instruct me" (see Job 42:2-6).

What was the pivotal moment of change for Job? He loved God, served Him, and lived a righteous life, yet faced tremendous loss and tragedy. In the aftermath of his personal devastation and pain, he confronted God but never cursed Him. God revealed Himself to this man. In response, Job said, "I have heard of You by the hearing of the ear; but now my eye sees You" (v. 6). Job went to a whole new level when he went from worshiping a God he had heard about to trusting a God he had seen. He got to the who, and it satisfied his questions.

Notice I didn't say that it answered his questions. God didn't describe what was going on in the spiritual realm. He didn't explain why He allowed those things to happen to Job. He didn't tell him when his suffering would end. He didn't tell him how to get healed or turn his situation around. He just told Job who He (God) was, and that was enough for this righteous man.

God gave Job seven more sons and three more daughters. He didn't just restore his wealth; he doubled it. Job lived to see four generations before dying "an old man and full of days" (Job 42:17 NASB).

This story of deep suffering drives home the proverb, "Trust in the Lord with all your heart; do not depend on your own understanding. Seek his will in all you do, and he will show you which path to take" (Proverbs 3:5-6 NLT). Merriam-Webster defines *trust* as "assured reliance on the character, ability, strength, or truth of someone or something." The connotation of the word in the Hebrew is to be confident, bold, and secure.

Back to the question: Do you trust God?

When you can't pay the bills or you get thrown out of your home, do you doubt God's desire to provide for you? Or do you hold to the assurance that God sees you and cares for you, no matter what happens? When you lose a loved one and don't understand why, do you question His character or rely on His unwavering goodness? When someone hurts you and never asks forgiveness, do you hold on to the bitterness and demand a reckoning? Or do you release the situation to Him with the confidence that His justice is superior to yours? When the diagnosis is hopeless, do you give in to despair or boldly battle the sickness while secure in the hope of eternity?

When we read God's response to Job's questions, it can seem harsh. But it's not a "who are you to question ME" kind of response. It's more like a sick child who doesn't understand why a painful needle does any good and a loving parent saying, "There's so much you don't know. Just trust me on this."

Job's story is unique. We should not expect the misery he faced. Instead, we should learn the truths that he discovered in his extreme situation. His friends offered explanations and advice based on their experiences, traditions, and human reasoning. They tried to explain things beyond their ability. All failed. Their best wisdom could not even begin to compare to the who of God. Job sought God, and He revealed Himself. Seeing God gave Job the peace, hope, comfort, and sanity that nothing else could. It enabled him to trust.

Trust does not eliminate the storms; it gives you an unsinkable boat to ride them out. It won't explain the waves, but it will deliver you safely to shore. When you don't understand what, when, why, or how, put your trust in the One who is beyond every question. We call God a supreme being because He is higher than anything we can fully grasp, yet He is a real and active entity. Trust His goodness, justice, mercy, power, and love. Most of all, trust in Him. You are far better for it.

DON'T QUOTE ME

By now, you probably realize that these upgrades in your thoughts, words, business, friends, family, works, and self are from the Bible, specifically the book of Proverbs. But here's the thing: Unless you're going to live these out, don't quote them. Just knowing it doesn't cut it.

Proverbs 26:7 says, "A proverb in the mouth of a fool is as useless as a paralyzed leg" (NLT). We have talked the talk, now it's time to walk the walk. Otherwise, you will just limp along through life, knowing what works, but not doing it.

James, the brother of Jesus, wrote, "...prove yourselves doers of the word, and not merely hearers who delude themselves. For if anyone is a hearer of the word and not a doer, he is like a man who looks at his natural face in a mirror; for once he has looked at himself and gone away, he has immediately forgotten what kind of person he was. But one who looks intently at the perfect law, the law of liberty, and abides by it, not having become a forgetful hearer but an effectual doer, this man will be blessed in what he does" (James 1:22-25 NASB).

You have the liberty to live by the truths in Scripture, or you can disregard them and live however you wish. If you want to receive the good things God wants to give you, follow the instructions He has laid out for us. He knows the road that leads to a good life, and He has mapped out the fastest way to get there. Take the shortcuts, and you'll enjoy a better life.

NOTES

NOTES

NOTES

NOTES

NOTES

NOTES

NOTES

NOTES

ENDNOTES

1. Dordick, Elliott. *Pitzer College RA: White People Can't Wear Hoop Earrings.* (2017, March 31). The Claremont Independent. http://claremontindependent.com/pitzer-college-ra-white-people-cant-wear-hoop-earrings/

2. Clarridge, Christine. *Judges complain it's unsafe, unsanitary outside King County Courthouse in Seattle.* (2017, July 18). Seattle Times. https://www.seattletimes.com/seattle-news/crime/judges-complain-its-unsafe-unsanitary-outside-county-courthouse-in-seattle/

3. Stelter, Brian and Liao, Shannon. *Disney, Netflix and WarnerMedia say new abortion law may push their movies out of Georgia.* (2019, May 30). CNN Business. https://www.cnn.com/2019/05/30/business/disney-bob-iger-abortion-georgia/index.html

4. Tamir, Diana I. and Mitchell, Jason P. *Disclosing information about the self is intrinsically rewarding.* (2012, May 7). PNAS. https://www.ncbi.nlm.nih.gov/pmc/articles/PMC3361411/

5. *How I Did It: Ralph Braun of BraunAbility.* (2009, December 1). Inc. https://www.inc.com/magazine/20091201/how-i-did-it-ralph-braun-of-braunability.html

6. *Jimmy Johnson's Life Is Football - And He Won't Let Anything Else Interfere.* (1993, January 24). Deseret News. https://www.deseret.com/1993/1/24/19028425/jimmy-johnson-s-life-is-football-and-he-won-t-let-anything-else-interfere

7. Nowak, Claire and Bare, Kelly. *Here's the Real Reason We Propose With Engagement Rings.* (2019, December 6). Reader's Digest. https://www.rd.com/advice/relationships/history-of-engagement-rings/

8. Baker, Aryn. *Blood Diamonds.* Time. https://time.com/blood-diamonds/

9. *Can relationships boost longevity and well-being?* (2017, June). Harvard Health Publishing: Harvard Medical School. https://www.health.harvard.edu/mental-health/can-relationships-boost-longevity-and-well-being

10. *Charles Darwin: Did He Help Create Scientific Racism?* (2009, February 12). Racism Review. http://www.racismreview.com/blog/2009/02/12/charles-darwin-did-he-help-create-scientific-racism/

11 Shurkin, Joel. *Scientific Consensus Is Almost Never Wrong — Almost.* (2015, November 20). Inside Science. https://www.insidescience.org/news/scientific-consensus-almost-never-wrong-—-almost

12. Watts, Anthony. *Al Gore's palm oil train wreck gets worse.* (2012, October 8). Watts Up With That? https://wattsupwiththat.com/2012/10/08/al-gores-palm-oil-train-wreck-gets-worse/

13. *Happiness Is a Moral Obligation*. The Dennis Prager
Show. (2007, February 20). https://www.dennisprager.com/
happiness-is-a-moral-obligation/

14. *Pain, anxiety, and depression: Why these conditions often
occur together and how to treat them when they do*. (2019,
June 5). Harvard Health Publishing: Harvard Medical
School. https://www.health.harvard.edu/mind-and-mood/pain-
anxiety-and-depression

15. TED. *How I climbed a 3,000-foot vertical cliff -- without
ropes | Alex Honnold* [Video]. (2018, October 29). YoutTube,
https://www.youtube.com/watch?v=6iM6M_7wBMc

16. Friedman, Matthew. *Just Facts: As Many Americans Have
Criminal Records as College Diplomas*. (2015, November 17).
Brennan Center for Justice. https://www.brennancenter.org/
our-work/analysis-opinion/just-facts-many-americans-have-
criminal-records-college-diplomas

17. King Jr., Martin Luther. (1958). Stride Toward Freedom:
The Montgomery Story. New York: Harper & Brothers).

18. Colby, Anne. *Meet the grandmother of memoir fabricators*. Los
Angeles Times. (2008, March 14). https://www.latimes.com/
archives/la-xpm-2008-mar-14-et-cradle14-story.html

19. HermitJim. *The Life Of Joan Lowell...!* Coffee with the
Hermit. (2018, September 18). https://hermitjim.blogspot.
com/2018/09/the-lie-of-joan-lowell.html

20. Moore, Cortney. *Giving Tuesday 2019 raised nearly $2B in donations*. Fox Business. (2019, December 5). https://www.foxbusiness.com/money/giving-tuesday-2019-raised-nearly-2b-in-donations

21. *Volunteers of various faiths helped clean up vandalized Jewish cemetery*. CBS News. (2017, February 28). https://www.cbsnews.com/news/volunteers-of-various-faiths-helped-clean-up-vandalized-jewish-cemetery/

22. Segal, Troy. *Enron Scandal: The Fall of a Wall Street Darling*. (2021, January 19). Investopedia. https://www.investopedia.com/updates/enron-scandal-summary/

23. *Enron, By The Numbers*. (2002, June 15). CBS News. https://www.cbsnews.com/news/enron-by-the-numbers/

24. *10 YEARS LATER: What Happened To The Former Employees Of Enron?* (2011, December 1). Insider. https://www.businessinsider.com/10-years-later-what-happened-to-the-former-employees-of-enron-2011-12